Savor THE Spirit

HERITAGE RECIPES
PASSED DOWN THROUGH THE YEARS

The Alabama Society
United States Daughters of 1812

Savor THE Spirit

HERITAGE RECIPES PASSED DOWN THROUGH THE YEARS

Published by The Alabama Society, United States Daughters of 1812

Library of Congress Control Number: 2002100988
ISBN: 0-9717624-0-6

Presidential portraits courtesy of the Library of Congress Archives

Edited, Designed, and Manufactured by
Favorite Recipes® Press
An imprint of

FRP

P. O. Box 305142
Nashville, Tennessee 37230
800-358-0560

Art Director: Steve Newman
Book Design: Starletta Polster
Project Editor: Linda Jones

Manufactured in the United States of America
First Printing: 2002   6,500 copies

 This symbol denotes heritage recipes.

About the Cover

Name of Painting: Flags

Date of Painting: 1918

Artist: Theodore Earl Butler (American)
1860–1936

Medium: Oil on canvas

*On loan to the Birmingham Museum of Art by an anonymous donor,
Birmingham, Alabama*

Contents

Preface

The founding fathers of our country set into motion a vision for the birth of a new nation with the Declaration of Independence written and signed on July 4, 1776. The following years were filled with turmoil and the sacrifices of life and fortunes as the war with Great Britain raged in our country. Their vision began to take shape as the Treaty of Paris was signed in 1783 by Great Britain, officially ending the Revolutionary War.

However, the vision was not a reality. The Continental Congress met at Annapolis, Maryland, and peace was proclaimed. The Treaty of Paris was ratified by Congress in 1784. Now it was necessary to have a centralized government if we were to protect our country from the many enemies both without and within. The Constitutional Convention met in Philadelphia in 1787. A constitution must be written and ratified, a governing body established, and treaties with other countries signed. George Washington was inaugurated as the first president of the United States with John Adams as his vice president in 1789. The new country was not at peace. There was war with the Indians, insurrections from our citizens, problems on the high seas with pirates, and Great Britain continued to capture our ships and men, forcing them into service for the British Navy. Congress authorized construction of six warships in 1794, thus founding the United States Navy, which had been defunct since 1775. The United States Navy frigates *Constitution*, *Constellation*, and *United States* came into service in 1797. The Navy Department was organized by an act of Congress in 1798. The nation expanded in size with the purchase of the Louisiana Territory from France in 1803, but the internal problems continued for the new country. The Lewis and Clark expedition began exploring the new territory. Disagreements escalated with Great Britain, which would lead to the War of 1812. Trade was discontinued with Britain in 1806, British ships were ordered out of American waters in 1807, in 1808 Napoleon ordered all United States ships in French ports seized and continued to do so through 1810, and war was declared on the Northwest Indians for a second time 1811–1813. The United States of America formally declared war against Great Britain in 1812. This war continued until a lasting peace was established on December 24, 1814, by the signing of the Treaty of Ghent with Great Britain at Ghent, Belgium. Thus the VISION of our founding fathers became a REALITY.

It is our desire that you will learn of an important time in our nation's history as you enjoy "celebrating the Birth of our Nation with cherished recipes from the past and present."

United States Daughters of 1812

The National Society United States Daughters of 1812 was organized on January 8, 1892, with Mrs. Flora Adams Darling as the founder and first president. The organizing president was Mrs. William Gerry Slade, who was president for eighteen years, 1897–1915. The first publication of the Society was reprinted in the December 1936 issue of the *News-Letter*. It sets forth the purpose and spirit of the Society.

The Regulations of the Society are set up in conformity with the period of our national history from the inception as a republic in 1784 through the War of 1812.

On February 25, 1901, the Society was incorporated by an Act of Congress (Public No. 86) and approved by President William McKinley at the National Society United States Daughters of Eighteen Hundred and Twelve. This was one of the first women's organizations to receive such a national charter. At the close of the administration of Mrs. William Gerry Slade in 1915, thirty-five state societies had been organized with an enrollment of 3,758 members.

The purposes of the United States Daughters of 1812 shall be to promote patriotism, to preserve and increase knowledge of the history of the American people by the preservation of documents and relics, the marking of historic spots, the recording of family histories and tradition, the celebration of patriotic anniversaries, teaching and emphasizing the heroic deeds of the civil, military, and naval life of those who molded this government between the close of the American Revolution and the close of the War of 1812, to urge Congress to compile and publish authentic records of men in civil, military, and naval service from 1784 to 1815 inclusive, to maintain at National Headquarters the library of memorabilia of the 1784–1815 period, and to assist in the care and maintenance of our "Real Granddaughters" in every way that will add to their comfort and happiness.

Savor the Spirit

The purpose of this cookbook is to raise funds

to fulfill the VISION of the

National Society of the United States Daughters of 1812's

dream of restoring the properties

owned by the National Society to have more

space for the Society's vast collection

of books in the Library and Museum collection

of artifacts and decorative arts.

Funds will go to finish this project thereby

making the VISION a REALITY.

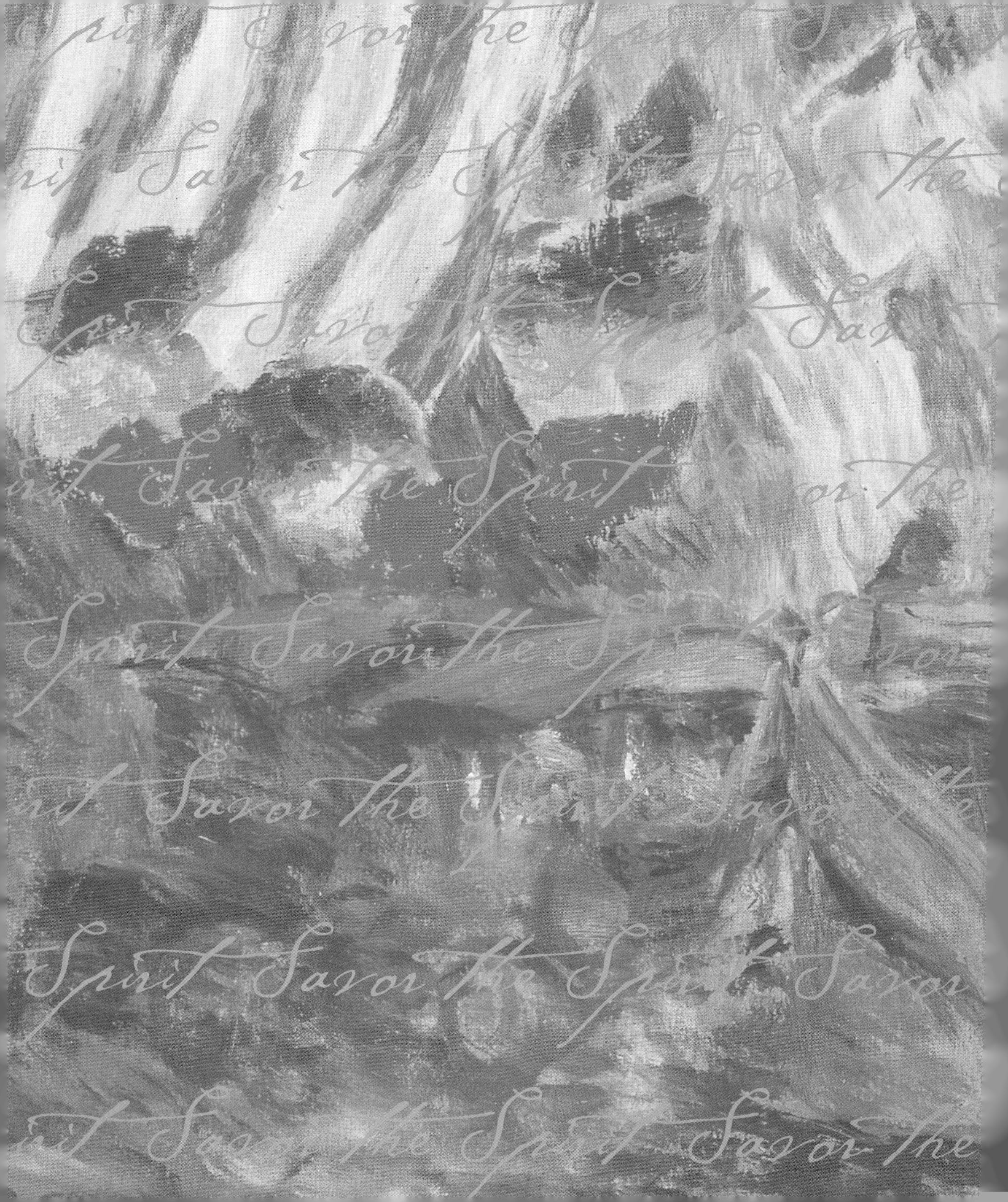
Savor the Spirit

First Courses

THE EARLY YEARS

1784–1788

Early American Buffet

Dolley Madison's Hospitable Bouillon

Thomas Jefferson's Okra Soup

Chowning's Tavern Brunswick Stew

Abigail Adams' Baked Salmon

George Washington's Indian Hoe Cakes

Martha Washington's Baked Indian Pudding

Thomas Jefferson's Potato Cakes

Thomas Jefferson's Sliced Apple Pudding

Thomas Jefferson's Vanilla Ice Cream

Monticello Toddy

American Revolution Cookies (Snickerdoodles)

Martha Washington's Rich Custard

Dolley Madison's Hospitable Bouillon

The hospitable and charming Dolley Madison is the most renowned hostess of all the presidential First Ladies. Dolley graciously welcomed everyone who visited the White House, and thereby gained a reputation for generous and warm hospitality. One of Dolley's most appreciated customs was serving her guests hot bouillon as they arrived and before they left when the weather was cold and dreary.

1 pound beef for stew	*1/2 cup snipped fresh parsley*
1 beef knuckle	*2 teaspoons salt*
1 cup chopped carrots	*1/8 teaspoon cayenne pepper*
1/2 cup chopped onion	*12 cups water*
1/2 cup chopped turnip	

Combine the beef, beef knuckle, carrots, onion, turnip, parsley, salt, cayenne pepper and water in a large saucepan or Dutch oven. Bring to a boil and reduce the heat. Simmer, covered, for 2 hours. Strain the broth, discarding the solids. Adjust the seasonings to taste. Serve hot.

YIELD: 10 SERVINGS

James Madison

Thomas Jefferson's Okra Soup

1 quart okra, trimmed, sliced
2 cups water
1 cup lima beans
1 pound beef, pork or chicken, cut up

5 tomatoes, chopped
Butter
Flour

Bring the okra and water to a boil in a saucepan. Cook for 30 minutes. Add the lima beans and beef. Cook until the beef is cooked through. Add the tomatoes. Cook for 1 hour. Roll butter the size of an egg in flour. Add to the soup. Simmer until thickened to the desired consistency, stirring frequently.

YIELD: 8 SERVINGS

Chowning's Tavern Brunswick Stew

6 pounds chicken
16 cups (1 gallon) water
2 cups lima beans
2 cups sliced okra (optional)
4 cups chopped peeled tomatoes
2 onions, sliced

4 medium potatoes, chopped
4 cups whole kernel corn
2 teaspoons salt
1/2 teaspoon pepper
1 tablespoon sugar

Cut the chicken into 8 pieces. Combine the chicken and water in a large stockpot. Simmer for 2 1/2 hours; do not boil. Remove the chicken to a platter. Chop the chicken, discarding the skin and bones. Add the lima beans, okra, tomatoes, onions and potatoes to the broth in the stockpot. Simmer until the lima beans are tender, adding additional hot water as necessary to prevent scorching. Add the corn, chicken, salt, pepper and sugar. Cook for 15 minutes or until the corn is tender.

YIELD: 12 SERVINGS

Abigail Adams' Baked Salmon

1 (4-pound) whole salmon
1 pint oysters
4 cups fresh bread crumbs
2 tablespoons butter, melted
2 eggs, beaten
1 tablespoon chopped fresh parsley

1/2 teaspoon thyme
1/2 teaspoon salt
Dash of pepper, ground cloves and grated
   nutmeg
2 cups dry red wine

Rinse the interior and exterior of the salmon well and pat dry. Drain the oysters, reserving 2 tablespoons of the liquor. Combine the bread crumbs, butter, eggs, parsley, thyme, salt, pepper, cloves and nutmeg in a bowl and mix well. Stir in the oysters and reserved liquor. Stuff into the salmon cavity. Arrange on a rack in a roasting pan. Pour the wine over the salmon. Butter one side of a sheet of parchment paper. Place buttered side down over the salmon. Bake at 500 degrees on the center oven rack for 10 minutes. Reduce the oven temperature to 425 degrees. Bake for 20 minutes. Remove the parchment paper. Bake for 10 minutes longer or until the salmon flakes easily. Serve with the pan drippings.

YIELD: 8 SERVINGS

John Adams

George Washington's Indian Hoe Cakes

George Washington liked to eat these with honey and tea for breakfast. The name derives from the original method of baking right on a hoe in the open hearth.

    1 cup water-ground white cornmeal   *1 tablespoon lard or shortening*
    1/2 teaspoon salt   *Boiling water*

Mix the cornmeal and salt in a bowl. Add the lard and enough boiling water to form a dough that will hold its shape. Shape the dough into 2 thin oblong cakes. Arrange in a hot well-greased heavy baking pan. Bake at 375 degrees for 25 minutes or until golden brown. Serve hot.

YIELD: 4 TO 6 SERVINGS

Martha Washington's Baked Indian Pudding

    1/3 cup cornmeal   *1/4 teaspoon ginger*
    1/2 cup molasses   *1/4 teaspoon cinnamon*
    Pinch of salt   *1/4 teaspoon nutmeg*
    3 cups scalded milk   *1 cup raisins*
    1 egg, beaten   *1 cup cold milk*

Combine the cornmeal, molasses and salt in a large bowl and mix well. Add 3 cups scalded milk. Let stand for 5 minutes. Add the egg, ginger, cinnamon and nutmeg and mix well. Stir in the raisins. Pour into a baking dish. Bake at 275 degrees for 10 minutes. Add 1 cup cold milk and stir to mix. Bake for 2 hours longer.

YIELD: 6 SERVINGS

George Washington

Thomas Jefferson's Potato Cakes

It is suspected that Thomas Jefferson tasted this type of recipe during a trip to Italy. This is a common recipe there, only the Italians shape the potatoes into small tubes 2¹/2 inches long and ³/4 inch wide.

*3 cups leftover mashed potatoes seasoned
    with butter, milk and salt
1¹/2 cups fresh bread crumbs*

*1 tablespoon butter
2 tablespoons vegetable oil
Salt and pepper to taste*

Shape the seasoned potatoes into 5 patties ¹/2 inch thick. Place the bread crumbs on a sheet of waxed paper. Coat the patties on both sides with the crumbs. Melt the butter with the oil in a large heavy skillet. Add the patties. Cook over low heat until golden brown on the bottom. Season with salt and pepper and turn. Cook until golden brown on the bottom.

YIELD: 5 SERVINGS

Thomas Jefferson's Sliced Apple Pudding

*3 apples, peeled, sliced
5 eggs
2 cups milk*

*Flour
Pinch of salt
3 tablespoons butter, melted*

Layer the apples in a baking dish. Beat the eggs in a mixing bowl until light. Add the milk and mix well. Add enough flour to form a medium-thick batter. Add the salt and butter and mix well. Pour over the apples. Bake at 350 degrees until set. Serve with sugar, melted butter and nutmeg.

YIELD: 4 SERVINGS

Note: You may use 5 peaches instead of the apples.

Thomas Jefferson's Vanilla Ice Cream

4 cups (1 quart) heavy cream
1 cup sugar
1/2 teaspoon salt

6 egg yolks
1 tablespoon vanilla extract

Combine the cream, sugar and salt in a heavy saucepan. Heat until bubbles just begin to appear, stirring frequently with a wooden spoon. Beat the egg yolks in a large mixing bowl. Add the cream mixture gradually in a fine stream, stirring constantly. Return to the saucepan. Cook over low heat until thickened, stirring constantly. Stir in the vanilla. Pour into an ice cream freezer container. Freeze using the manufacturer's directions.

YIELD: 8 SERVINGS

Monticello Toddy

Jefferson's recipe was later used by other United States presidents, especially Dwight Eisenhower.

1¹/2 cups sugar
1 cup brandy
1 cup dark rum
1 cup dry sherry
1 cup madeira
1/4 cup anisette liqueur

1/4 cup peach brandy
1/4 cup orange liqueur
Dash of grated nutmeg
4 cups (1 quart) apple cider
Dry or fresh apple rings

Combine the sugar, brandy, rum, sherry, madeira, anisette liqueur, peach brandy, orange liqueur, nutmeg, apple cider and apple rings in a large container and mix well. Chill, covered, for 8 to 12 hours. Strain into a punch bowl, discarding the solids. Garnish with additional apple rings and nutmeg.

YIELD: 12 (6-OUNCE) SERVINGS

Thomas Jefferson

American Revolution Cookies (Snickerdoodles)

2³/4 cups flour
2 teaspoons cream of tartar
1 teaspoon baking soda
1/4 teaspoon salt
1/2 cup (1 stick) butter, softened
1/2 cup shortening

1¹/2 cups sugar
2 eggs
1 teaspoon vanilla extract
2 tablespoons sugar
1 tablespoon cinnamon

Mix the flour, cream of tartar, baking soda and salt together in a bowl. Cream the butter, shortening and 1¹/2 cups sugar in a mixing bowl until light and fluffy. Add the eggs and vanilla and beat until smooth. Add the flour mixture and beat well. Mix 2 tablespoons sugar and the cinnamon in a small bowl. Shape the dough into 1-inch balls. Roll in the sugar mixture to coat. Arrange on a silpat-lined or greased cookie sheet. Bake at 400 degrees for 10 minutes.

YIELD: 5 1/2 DOZEN

Martha Washington's Rich Custard

4 cups (1 quart) milk
1/2 cup sugar
Pinch of salt

6 eggs
1/2 cup cold milk
1/4 teaspoon vanilla or almond extract

Scald 4 cups milk in a double boiler over boiling water. Add the sugar and salt and mix well. Beat the eggs in a mixing bowl. Add 1/2 cup cold milk and beat well. Add to the hot milk mixture gradually, stirring constantly. Cook until thickened and the mixture coats a spoon, stirring constantly. Remove from the heat. Let stand until cool. Stir in the vanilla.

YIELD: 8 SERVINGS

1784

Congress ratified the Treaty of Paris between the United States and England.

Spain took possession of St. Augustine, Florida.

The first major depression occurred in the United States (1784–1789).

Spain informed the United States that American ships on the Mississippi River in Spanish territory would be seized.

North Carolina offered to cede all of its western lands to the federal government.

The first daily newspaper in America, the *American Daily Advertiser*, was published in Philadelphia.

The first law school in the United States was established in Litchfield, Connecticut.

Simple Three-Cheese Ball

8 ounces cream cheese, softened
1 (5-ounce) jar Old English cheese spread
4 to 6 ounces bleu cheese, crumbled
Garlic salt to taste
1 cup toasted pecans, finely chopped

Combine the cream cheese, cheese spread and bleu cheese in a large bowl. Let stand until softened. Sprinkle with garlic salt. Mix until smooth. Shape into a ball. Roll in the pecans. Wrap in plastic wrap. Chill, covered, for 8 to 12 hours before serving.

YIELD: 8 SERVINGS

Pineapple Cheese Ball

16 ounces cream cheese, softened
1/4 cup finely chopped green bell pepper
1/4 cup finely chopped onion
1 tablespoon seasoned salt
1 (8-ounce) can crushed pineapple,
   drained
2 cups finely chopped pecans

Combine the cream cheese, bell pepper, onion, seasoned salt, pineapple and 3/4 cup of the pecans in a large bowl and mix well. Shape into 1 or 2 balls. Roll in the remaining pecans. Serve with wheat crackers or assorted crackers.

YIELD: 12 SERVINGS

Easy Cheese Dip

1 cup grated cheese
1 cup mayonnaise

1 cup minced onion

Combine the cheese, mayonnaise and onion in a bowl and mix well. Spoon into a baking dish. Bake at 350 degrees until bubbly. Serve with assorted crackers or chips.

YIELD: 3 CUPS

Shrimp Dip

8 ounces cream cheese, softened
1 (4-ounce) can shrimp pieces, drained
1 tablespoon lemon juice

1 teaspoon Worcestershire sauce
1 teaspoon garlic salt
2 tablespoons milk

Process the cream cheese, shrimp, lemon juice, Worcestershire sauce, garlic salt and milk in a blender until blended. Spoon into a serving bowl. Chill, covered, for a few hours or longer before serving.

YIELD: 8 SERVINGS

Note: You may use small frozen shrimp instead of the canned shrimp.

Southwestern Dip

1 pound ground beef, cooked, drained
1 pound Velveeta cheese, melted

1 (16-ounce) jar salsa

Combine the ground beef, Velveeta cheese and salsa in a bowl and mix well. Serve warm with tortilla chips.

YIELD: 12 SERVINGS

Hot Beef Spread

1/2 cup chopped onion
1 tablespoon butter
2 tablespoons dry white wine
8 ounces cream cheese, softened
1/2 cup sour cream

1/2 cup mayonnaise
1 (2-ounce) jar dried beef, finely chopped
1 tablespoon Worcestershire sauce
1/2 cup chopped pecans

Sauté the onion in the butter in a skillet until tender. Stir in the wine. Simmer for 2 minutes. Add the cream cheese, sour cream, mayonnaise, dried beef and Worcestershire sauce and mix well. Spoon into an 8×8-inch baking dish. Sprinkle with the pecans. Bake at 350 degrees for 20 minutes or until hot and bubbly. Serve with assorted crackers.

YIELD: 12 SERVINGS

Crowded Elaborate Tables

Crowded elaborate tables had been a mark of status in England since the early fifteenth century when the king and princes of the church had competed with each other to demonstrate their wealth and power. The aristocracy copied royalty and nobility; wealthy merchants and lesser folk aped the aristocracy. Through the centuries, a great display of food and a rich setting for it had been a measure of man's position in society.

Artichoke Hearts in Bleu Cheese

6 (14-ounce) cans whole artichoke hearts
4 ounces bleu cheese, crumbled
3/4 cup (1 1/2 sticks) butter
2 tablespoons lemon juice

Drain the artichoke hearts and cut into quarters. Melt the bleu cheese and butter in a saucepan. Stir in the lemon juice. Spoon into a chafing dish. Add 1/3 of the artichoke heart quarters. Replenish with the remaining artichoke heart quarters as needed. Use wooden picks to serve.

YIELD: 20 SERVINGS

Hot Crab Crisps

3 or 4 French bread hoagie buns, chilled
1 cup mayonnaise
1/2 cup finely chopped green onions
1 cup freshly shredded Parmesan cheese
4 drops of Tabasco sauce
1 tablespoon fresh lemon juice
8 ounces fresh crab meat

Cut the buns into thin round slices about 1/4 inch thick. Arrange on a baking sheet. Bake at 300 degrees for 10 minutes or until crisp. Remove from the oven. Combine the mayonnaise, green onions, Parmesan cheese, Tabasco sauce and lemon juice in a small bowl and mix well. Fold in the crab meat. Spread on the bread rounds. Increase the oven temperature to 350 degrees. Bake for 15 minutes or until bubbly and light brown. Garnish with chopped fresh parsley.

YIELD: 50 TO 55 ROUNDS

1785

Thomas Jefferson proposed a coinage system to Congress.

John Adams became the first United States envoy to England.

Congress adopted the decimal system for money, with the dollar as the unit.

Benjamin Franklin and Adams concluded a treaty of amity and commerce with Prussia.

Thomas Jefferson succeeded Franklin as minister to France.

Congress first provided for carrying mail by stagecoach.

The United States concluded a treaty with the Cherokee Indians.

Hot Ham Sandwiches

Excellent to make for a tailgating party.

1 small onion, chopped
1 cup (2 sticks) margarine
1/3 cup Grey Poupon mustard
1 teaspoon poppy seeds

2 (16-ounce) packages sliced ham,
  shredded
8 hamburger buns, split
8 slices Swiss cheese

Sauté the onion in the margarine in a skillet until tender. Add the mustard, poppy seeds and ham and mix well. Spread 3 tablespoons of the ham mixture on the bottom half of each bun. Top each with a slice of Swiss cheese. Replace the bun tops. Wrap each in foil and place on a baking sheet. Bake at 350 degrees until heated through.

YIELD: 8 SANDWICHES

Note: You may make ahead and freeze. Thaw and bake before serving. Use dinner rolls if you wish to serve as finger sandwiches.

Bridge Mix

2 (10-ounce) packages oyster crackers
1/2 cup vegetable oil
1/2 teaspoon garlic salt

1 teaspoon dillweed
1 envelope ranch salad dressing mix

Combine the crackers, oil, garlic salt, dillweed and dressing mix in a large bowl and stir to mix well. Let stand and then stir again. Repeat until all of the oil mixture is absorbed. Store in a sealable plastic bag for several days before serving.

YIELD: 20 SERVINGS

Party Fruit Punch

4 cups hot strong brewed tea
2 cups sugar
4 cups apple or pineapple juice
1 (6-ounce) can frozen lemonade
  concentrate, prepared

1 (6-ounce) can frozen orange juice
  concentrate, prepared
2 quarts sparkling water
1 (4-ounce) jar maraschino cherries

Pour the hot tea over the sugar in a large container and stir until the sugar is dissolved. Let stand until cool. Add the apple juice, lemonade and orange juice and mix well. Store, covered, in large glass jars in the refrigerator for 3 to 4 days before serving. Add the sparkling water and undrained cherries just before serving.

YIELD: 24 SERVINGS

Eggnog

6 egg yolks
6 tablespoons sugar
12 ounces bourbon

6 egg whites
1 cup whipping cream, whipped

Beat the egg yolks and sugar in a large mixing bowl until pale yellow. Stir in the bourbon. Beat the egg whites in a separate mixing bowl until stiff peaks form. Fold into the egg yolk mixture. Fold in the whipped cream. Ladle into serving cups.

YIELD: 6 SERVINGS

Christmas Cranberry Punch

Heat 4 cups cranberry juice cocktail, 4 cups apple juice, juice of 2 oranges, 2 tablespoons sugar, 2 cinnamon sticks and 8 whole cloves in a large saucepan over low heat. Ladle into serving cups. Garnish with lemon or lime slices studded with whole cloves.

Quick Artichoke Soup

1 bunch green onions, finely chopped
1 onion, finely chopped
Chopped fresh parsley to taste
1/4 cup (1/2 stick) butter

2 (14-ounce) cans artichoke hearts
1 (10-ounce) can cream of mushroom
 soup
1 soup can milk

Sauté the green onions, onion and parsley in the butter in a skillet until tender. Add the undrained artichoke hearts and mix well. Stir in the mushroom soup and milk. Simmer for 30 minutes, stirring frequently and adding additional milk if needed for the desired consistency. Ladle into soup bowls.

YIELD: 8 SERVINGS

Note: You may add crab meat for a heartier soup.

Creamy Cauliflower Soup

1 medium head cauliflower, cut into
 florets
1 cup chopped onion
1/2 cup chopped celery
2 (14-ounce) cans chicken broth

1/2 teaspoon Worcestershire sauce
1/2 cup water
1 teaspoon salt
1/8 teaspoon pepper
1 1/2 cups light cream or evaporated milk

Combine the cauliflower, onion, celery, broth, Worcestershire sauce, water, salt and pepper in a large saucepan. Bring to a boil over medium heat. Reduce the heat and cover. Simmer for 13 minutes or until the vegetables are tender. Purée a small amount at a time in a blender. Return to the saucepan. Stir in the cream. Cook for 2 minutes or until heated through. Ladle into soup bowls.

YIELD: 6 SERVINGS

Vichyssoise (Potato Soup)

4 leeks, or 1¹/2 cups minced onions
3 cups chopped peeled potatoes
3 cups boiling water
4 chicken bouillon cubes
3 tablespoons butter or margarine
1 cup light cream, heavy cream or
*   evaporated milk*
1 cup milk
1 teaspoon salt
¹/4 teaspoon white pepper
2 tablespoons minced fresh chives, or
*   ¹/4 teaspoon paprika*

Rinse the leeks. Cut the leeks and about 3 of the green tops into fine pieces. Combine the leeks, potatoes and boiling water in a saucepan. Cook, covered, for 20 minutes or until tender. Press the undrained mixture through a ricer into a double boiler. Add the bouillon cubes and mash well. Add the butter, cream, milk, salt and white pepper and mix well. Cook until heated through and blended, stirring constantly. Pour into a bowl. Chill, covered, for 8 to 12 hours. Serve cold sprinkled with chives or reheat and serve hot sprinkled with chives.

YIELD: 9 SERVINGS

1786

James Madison was appointed to the Virginia Legislature.

Congress passed an ordinance establishing the United States Mint.

Cleveland, Ohio, was established as a trading post.

The United States signed a treaty with the Choctaw, Chickasaw, and Shawnee Indians.

Congress demanded that Spain grant the United States shipping rights on the Mississippi River.

The first known Sunday school in America was established in Hanover County, Virginia.

Tomato Orange Soup

2 (10-ounce) cans tomato or Italian
   tomato soup
1 soup can water
1 tablespoon Worcestershire sauce

1 (6-ounce) can orange juice
1/2 teaspoon basil
1/4 teaspoon salt
Coarsely ground pepper to taste

Combine the tomato soup, water, Worcestershire sauce, orange juice, basil, salt and pepper in a saucepan. Bring to a boil, stirring constantly. Cook until heated through. Ladle into soup bowls. Garnish each serving with a small slice of orange topped with a dollop of sour cream and a sprig of fresh basil or parsley.

YIELD: 8 SERVINGS

Cherry Pineapple Salad

1 (20-ounce) can crushed pineapple
1 (16-ounce) can Bing cherries
1 (12-ounce) can cola

2 (3-ounce) packages cherry gelatin
1 cup chopped toasted pecans

Drain the pineapple and cherries, reserving the juice. Bring the reserved juice to a boil in a saucepan. Stir in the cola. Add the gelatin. Heat until the gelatin dissolves, stirring constantly. Remove from the heat. Stir in the pineapple, cherries and pecans. Pour into a lightly greased 8×8-inch dish. Chill, covered, until firm.

YIELD: 8 TO 10 SERVINGS

Fruit Salad

1 (20-ounce) can juice-pack
    pineapple chunks
1 cup sugar
2 tablespoons flour
Pinch of salt
2 eggs
2 tablespoons butter
1 cup sliced banana, or to taste
1 cup miniature marshmallows,
    or to taste
1/4 cup chopped toasted pecans,
    or to taste

Drain the pineapple, reserving 1 cup of the juice. Mix the sugar, flour and salt together. Combine the reserved juice, eggs and butter in a saucepan and mix well. Stir in the sugar mixture gradually. Cook over low heat until thickened and bubbly, stirring constantly. Remove from the heat. Chill, covered, in the refrigerator.

Combine the pineapple, banana, marshmallows and pecans in a large bowl. Add the chilled mixture and toss to coat.

YIELD: 8 SERVINGS

1787

The Constitutional Convention met in Philadelphia.

George Washington was elected president of the Constitutional Convention.

Delegates to the convention signed the Constitution, as amended, and were adjourned.

Delaware became the first state to ratify the Constitution, followed by Pennsylvania and New Jersey.

The *Columbia*, the first ship to carry the United States flag around the world, left Boston.

Orange Salad Ambrosia

1 (3-ounce) package orange gelatin
1 cup boiling water
1 cup sour cream
3 tablespoons sugar

1 cup drained crushed pineapple
1 cup mandarin orange sections
1/2 cup shredded coconut
1/2 cup chopped pecans

Dissolve the gelatin in the boiling water in a mixing bowl. Chill until the consistency of unbeaten egg whites. Beat at low speed for 1 minute or until smooth. Beat in the sour cream and sugar until blended. Fold in the pineapple, orange sections, coconut and pecans. Pour into a salad mold. Chill until firm. Unmold onto a serving plate.

YIELD: 6 SERVINGS

Note: This recipe may be doubled.

Tomato Aspic

1 (6-ounce) package lemon gelatin
1 1/4 cups boiling water
2 (8-ounce) cans tomato sauce
3 tablespoons vinegar
1 teaspoon salt

1 teaspoon onion juice or grated onion
Dash of ground cloves
2 or 3 tablespoons mild salsa
2 or 3 cups sliced celery

Dissolve the gelatin in the boiling water in a bowl. Add the tomato sauce, vinegar, salt, onion juice and cloves. Chill until partially set. Stir in the salsa and celery. Pour into a ring mold or glass dish. Chill until set. Unmold onto a serving plate.

YIELD: 12 SERVINGS

Spinach Salad

1/2 cup sugar
1 tablespoon sesame seeds
1 tablespoon poppy seeds
1 1/2 teaspoons minced onion
1/4 teaspoon Worcestershire sauce
1/4 teaspoon paprika
1/2 cup white wine vinegar
1/2 cup vegetable oil
1 large bunch fresh spinach, rinsed,
  trimmed
1 pint strawberries, rinsed, trimmed,
  sliced
1/2 cup walnuts, toasted, chopped
1/2 cup crumbled bleu cheese

Process the sugar, sesame seeds, poppy seeds, onion, Worcestershire sauce, paprika, vinegar and oil in a blender or food processor until the sugar dissolves. Layer the spinach, strawberries, walnuts and bleu cheese in a large salad bowl in the order listed. Drizzle with the dressing.

YIELD: 8 SERVINGS

1788

The last Congress of the Confederation met in New York. Afterwards, it became the United States Congress.

Georgia, Connecticut, Massachusetts, Maryland, South Carolina, New Hampshire, and New York ratified the Constitution.

The District of Columbia, Washington City, was established under the Constitution.

Andrew Jackson moved to Nashville, Tennessee, and began a law practice.

Cotton was first planted in Georgia.

The first trotting horses were imported to the United States.

The practice of surgical dissection provoked serious rioting in New York City.

Cranberry Broccoli Salad

1 1/4 cups fresh cranberries, chopped
1/4 cup sugar
1/3 cup light mayonnaise
1/4 cup sugar
1 tablespoon vinegar
4 cups broccoli florets (2 bunches)

4 cups coleslaw with carrots mix
1/2 cup chopped pecans
1/2 cup raisins
1/3 cup chopped onion
6 slices bacon, cooked, drained, crumbled

Combine the cranberries and 1/4 cup sugar in a small bowl and toss to mix well. Chill, covered, until ready to assemble the salad.

Mix the mayonnaise, 1/4 cup sugar and vinegar in a small bowl. Combine the broccoli, coleslaw mix, pecans, raisins, onion and bacon in a large bowl and toss to mix. Add the dressing and toss to coat. Chill, covered, for 8 to 12 hours. Add the cranberry mixture just before serving and toss gently.

YIELD: 8 TO 10 SERVINGS

Marinated Cauliflower Tossed Salad

1/2 cup vegetable oil
1/4 cup vinegar
Chopped olives to taste
1 medium purple onion, chopped

1 head cauliflower, cut into florets
1 head lettuce, rinsed, drained
Crumbled bleu cheese to taste
Cooked crumbled bacon to taste

Blend the oil and vinegar in a large bowl. Add the olives, onion and cauliflower and toss to coat. Marinate, covered, in the refrigerator for 8 to 12 hours. Tear the lettuce into bite-size pieces into a large salad bowl. Add the cauliflower mixture and toss to mix. Chill, covered, for 1 hour. Sprinkle with the bleu cheese and bacon just before serving.

YIELD: 8 SERVINGS

Calico Salad

1 (11-ounce) can white Shoe Peg corn
1 (16-ounce) can French-style green beans
1 (16-ounce) can green peas
1 (2-ounce) jar pimento
1 cup chopped carrots
1 cup chopped celery
1/2 cup chopped onion

1/4 cup chopped green bell pepper
1 cup sugar
3/4 cup vinegar
1/2 cup vegetable oil
1 tablespoon water
1/2 teaspoon salt
Pepper to taste

Drain the corn, green beans, green peas and pimento in a colander for 2 hours. Combine with the carrots, celery, onion and bell pepper in a large bowl and mix well. Bring the sugar, vinegar, oil, water, salt and pepper to a boil in a saucepan. Pour over the vegetables. Chill, covered, for 8 to 12 hours.

YIELD: 6 TO 8 SERVINGS

Note: You may store for several days in the refrigerator.

Main Dishes

THE WASHINGTON YEARS
1789–1796

Stuffed Beef Tenderloin

1/4 cup (1/2 stick) butter
1 medium onion, chopped
1/2 cup chopped celery
1 (4-ounce) can sliced mushrooms,
    drained
2 cups soft bread crumbs

1/2 teaspoon salt
1/4 teaspoon pepper
1/2 teaspoon basil
1/2 teaspoon parsley flakes
3 pounds beef tenderloin
4 slices bacon

Melt the butter in a small skillet over low heat. Add the onion, celery and mushrooms. Sauté for 10 minutes or until the onion is transparent. Combine the bread crumbs, salt, pepper, basil and parsley flakes in a 1-quart bowl. Add the onion mixture and mix lightly to blend.

Cut the tenderloin lengthwise 3/4 of the way through. Pack the stuffing into the pocket. Close the pocket using wooden picks. Arrange the bacon slices diagonally across the top to cover the wooden picks and pocket. Arrange the stuffed tenderloin in a 10×13-inch baking dish. Bake, uncovered, at 350 degrees for 1 hour for medium-rare.

YIELD: 8 SERVINGS

George Washington
George Washington, a military man of many years, was elected to the Virginia House of Burgesses in 1759 and settled into the life of a gentleman farmer after he married. However, he risked it all by casting his lot with those rebelling against the British rule. He took command of the Virginia militia and the next year was appointed commander and chief of the Continental army. He was a popular general among his soldiers and led them across the Delaware to rout the enemy at Trenton. He held his army together despite severe conditions at Valley Forge in 1777–78. Later, in 1781, he led his army to victory at Yorktown. This effectively ended the war. He was elected the first president in 1789.

Buffet Beef Surprise

This recipe is from a collection of old Stroud family recipes called Not a Bad One in the Bunch. *The Strouds lived in Kinston, North Carolina.*

1 (3-pound) boneless chuck roast
2 (16-ounce) cans sauerkraut, drained
1 (1-pound) package dark brown sugar

1 (18-ounce) can whole tomatoes
1 onion, sliced
1 apple, peeled, sliced

Arrange the beef in a baking dish with a tight-fitting lid. Layer the sauerkraut, brown sugar, undrained tomatoes, onion slices and apple slices over the beef. Bake, tightly covered, at 325 degrees for 3½ to 4 hours or until the beef falls apart.

YIELD: 8 SERVINGS

Steaks with Sautéed Onions

4 tenderloin steaks, cut 1 inch thick
¼ teaspoon salt
¼ teaspoon pepper
2 tablespoons margarine

1 large Vidalia or Spanish onion,
    cut into 10 wedges
3 garlic cloves, minced
1 teaspoon basil
¼ cup heavy cream or half-and-half

Sprinkle the steaks with salt and pepper. Melt the margarine in a large heavy skillet over medium heat. Add the onion and garlic. Sauté until tender, but not brown. Remove from the skillet. Increase the heat to medium-high. Add the steaks to the skillet. Cook for 4 minutes on each side for rare or to the desired degree of doneness, turning once. Sprinkle with basil. Remove from the skillet and keep warm. Return the onion mixture to the skillet. Cook until heated through. Stir in the cream. Spoon over the steaks.

YIELD: 4 SERVINGS

Standing Rib Roast

1 (6-pound) standing rib roast
1 teaspoon kosher salt
1 teaspoon freshly ground pepper

Sprinkle the roast with kosher salt and pepper. Arrange fat side up on a lightly greased rack in a foil-lined roasting pan. Bake, uncovered, at 350 degrees for 2 hours or until a meat thermometer inserted into the thickest portion registers 145 degrees for medium-rare. Remove the roast to a serving platter, reserving 1/2 cup of the pan juices. Let stand for 10 minutes before carving. Serve with the reserved pan juices.

YIELD: 8 SERVINGS

Chili

1 1/2 pounds ground beef
2 (20-ounce) cans tomatoes
2 (20-ounce) cans New Orleans-style
    kidney beans
1 large onion, chopped
3 tablespoons chili powder
Salt and pepper to taste
1 green bell pepper, chopped
1 small hot pepper, chopped (optional)

Brown the ground beef in a skillet, stirring until crumbly; drain. Combine the ground beef, tomatoes, kidney beans, onion, chili powder, salt, pepper, bell pepper and hot pepper in a Dutch oven. Cook over medium-low heat for 1 1/2 hours or until ready to serve.

YIELD: 4 SERVINGS

Note: You may double the recipe and store the remaining chili in a freezer container for a future meal.

1789

George Washington was inaugurated as the first president of the United States. John Adams was his vice president.

North Carolina became the twelfth state to ratify the Constitution.

The State Department, the United States Treasury, and the War Department were created.

John Jay became the first chief justice of the United States Supreme Court.

James Madison sponsored the Bill of Rights.

Chunky Italian Soup

1 pound ground beef or beef tips
1 medium onion, chopped
2 (14-ounce) cans Italian tomatoes
1 (10-ounce) can tomato soup with basil
4 cups water
2 garlic cloves, minced
2 teaspoons basil
2 teaspoons oregano
1 teaspoon salt

^{1}/2 teaspoon pepper
1 tablespoon chili powder (optional)
1 (16-ounce) can kidney beans, drained
1 (16-ounce) can Italian green beans,
   drained
1 carrot, chopped
1 zucchini, chopped
8 ounces rotini, cooked
Grated Parmesan cheese

Brown the ground beef and onion in a Dutch oven over medium heat, stirring until the ground beef is crumbly; drain. Add the undrained tomatoes, tomato soup, water, garlic, basil, oregano, salt, pepper and chili powder and mix well. Bring to a boil and reduce the heat. Simmer for 30 minutes, stirring occasionally. Stir in the kidney beans, green beans, carrot and zucchini. Simmer for 15 minutes, stirring occasionally. Stir in the cooked pasta. Ladle into soup bowls. Sprinkle with Parmesan cheese.

YIELD: 10 SERVINGS

Roast "Lion"

Roast "Lion" is said to be Amish in origin. The flavors of the two kinds of meat intermingle to create a delicious new taste. To prepare, use equal portions of any cut of beef and pork roast, allowing 4 ounces each of the beef and pork per serving. Arrange the beef and pork in a roasting pan. Bake, covered, at 325 degrees for 35 minutes per pound of pork or until the pork is cooked through. The beef will be well done but not dry. Remove the beef and pork to a serving platter. Cut into slices. Make a gravy using the pan juices and serve over noodles or mashed potatoes with the beef and pork slices.

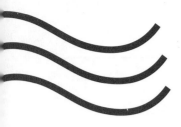

1790

Congress met in New York to hear President Washington give his first annual address.

Rhode Island ratified the Constitution.

Congress authorized the first census. The population was placed at 3,929,625.

Thomas Jefferson became the first secretary of state.

Benjamin Franklin died in Philadelphia at the age of 84.

Santa Fe Soup

2 pounds ground turkey or ground beef
1 onion, chopped
2 envelopes ranch salad dressing mix
2 envelopes taco seasoning mix
1 (16-ounce) can black beans
1 (16-ounce) can kidney beans
1 (16-ounce) can pinto beans
1 (16-ounce) can diced tomatoes
  with chiles
1 (16-ounce) can tomato wedges
2 (16-ounce) cans whole kernel white corn
2 cups water

Brown the ground turkey with the onion in a skillet, stirring until the ground turkey is crumbly; drain. Add the salad dressing mix and taco seasoning mix and mix well. Add the undrained vegetables and water.

Bring to a boil and reduce the heat. Simmer for 2 hours, adding additional water if needed for the desired consistency. Ladle into soup bowls. Garnish with sour cream, shredded Cheddar cheese and sliced green onions. Serve with tortilla chips.

YIELD: 16 SERVINGS

Easy Lasagna

1 pound ground beef
3 1/2 cups thick spaghetti sauce
1 1/2 cups water
2 cups ricotta cheese or small curd
  cottage cheese
3 cups shredded mozzarella cheese
1/2 cup grated Parmesan cheese
2 eggs
1/4 cup chopped fresh parsley
1 teaspoon salt
1/4 teaspoon pepper
8 ounces uncooked lasagna noodles

Brown the ground beef in a skillet, stirring until crumbly. Add the spaghetti sauce and water. Bring to a boil and reduce the heat. Simmer for 10 minutes. Combine the ricotta cheese, mozzarella cheese, Parmesan cheese, eggs, parsley, salt and pepper in a bowl and mix well. Pour 1 cup of the ground beef mixture into a 9×13-inch baking dish. Layer the lasagna noodles, the remaining ground beef mixture and the cheese mixture 1/2 at a time in the prepared dish. Bake, covered with foil, for 55 to 60 minutes or until bubbly. Bake, uncovered, for 10 minutes longer.

YIELD: 8 TO 10 SERVINGS

1790

The Federal Naturalization Act was passed by Congress.

A war with the Northwest Indians began.

Philadelphia was the largest city and Virginia was the most populous state.

Duncan Phyfe, a Scottish immigrant, opened a chair shop in New York.

The first American ship to sail around the world, the *Columbia*, returned to Boston.

Taco Salad

1 pound ground round
1 (16-ounce) can kidney beans, drained
3 green onions, chopped
3 small tomatoes, chopped
1 (2-ounce) can sliced black olives,
  drained

1 head lettuce
2 cups shredded Cheddar cheese
1/2 (16-ounce) bottle Thousand Island
  salad dressing
1 (8-ounce) package cheesy Doritos,
  crumbled

Brown the ground round in a large skillet, stirring until crumbly; drain. Remove from the heat. Add the kidney beans, green onions, tomatoes and black olives and mix well. Rinse the lettuce and pat dry. Tear into bite-size pieces into a large serving bowl. Add the ground round mixture, Cheddar cheese and salad dressing and toss to mix. Sprinkle with the chips.

YIELD: 6 SERVINGS

Ground Beef Noodle Stroganoff

1 pound ground beef
1/2 cup chopped onion
1 (10-ounce) can cream of mushroom
  soup
1/2 cup sour cream
1/2 cup water

1/2 teaspoon salt
1/8 teaspoon pepper
1/2 teaspoon paprika (optional)
2 cups cooked noodles
Sliced tomatoes
Buttered bread crumbs

Brown the ground beef with the onion in a skillet, stirring until the ground beef is crumbly and cooking until the onion is tender; drain. Add the soup, sour cream, water, salt, pepper, paprika and noodles and mix well. Spoon into a greased 1 1/2-quart shallow baking dish. Bake at 400 degrees for 25 minutes. Remove from the oven and stir. Top with sliced tomatoes and sprinkle with buttered bread crumbs. Bake for 5 minutes.

YIELD: 4 SERVINGS

Spicy Meat Loaf

1 pound ground beef
8 ounces lean hot sausage
1/2 large onion, minced
1 rib celery, chopped
1 egg, beaten
1 teaspoon MSG
1/4 teaspoon garlic salt
1/2 teaspoon salt
1/2 teaspoon pepper
6 ounces chili sauce
1/4 cup milk
1 cup herb-seasoned stuffing mix
Tomato Sauce (below)

Combine the ground beef, sausage, onion, celery, egg, MSG, garlic salt, salt, pepper, chili sauce, milk and stuffing mix in a large bowl and mix well using your hands. Shape into a loaf. Press into a greased 5×9-inch loaf pan. Bake at 350 degrees for 1 hour. Remove from the oven and pour off the excess grease. Spread the Tomato Sauce over the top. Bake for 15 minutes or until cooked through.

YIELD: 8 SERVINGS

Tomato Sauce

1 (16-ounce) can chopped tomatoes
1 (6-ounce) can tomato paste
2 tablespoons minced onion
2 teaspoons oregano

Combine the tomatoes, tomato paste, onion and oregano in a bowl and mix well.

YIELD: ABOUT 3 CUPS

1791

Vermont became the fourteenth state.

President Washington initiated the custom of a presidential New Year's Day reception at the Executive Mansion. This practice was suspended by Franklin Roosevelt in 1934.

President Washington's practice of consulting regularly with his department secretaries gave rise to the presidential "cabinet," an official group of trusted advisors.

Coal was discovered in Carbon County, Pennsylvania.

The first sugar refinery opened in New Orleans.

Double Fruit-Glazed Pork Chops

6 (6- to 8-ounce) double-rib pork chops
Vegetable oil
Salt and pepper to taste
2 cups packed brown sugar
1/2 cup unsweetened pineapple juice
1/2 cup honey
2 teaspoons dry mustard

6 whole cloves
12 whole coriander seeds, crushed
6 orange slices
6 lemon slices
6 lime slices
6 maraschino cherries
Honeyed Bananas (below)

Brown the pork chops in a small amount of oil in a skillet. Season with salt and pepper. Arrange in a shallow baking pan. Mix the brown sugar, pineapple juice, honey, dry mustard, cloves and coriander seeds in a bowl. Spoon about 3 tablespoons of the sauce over each pork chop. Bake, uncovered, at 350 degrees for 1 1/4 hours or until cooked through, basting occasionally with the remaining sauce. Skewer an orange slice, lemon slice and lime slice on each of six wooden picks. Top each with a maraschino cherry. Insert one skewer into each pork chop and baste with the sauce. Bake for 10 minutes longer. Arrange the pork chops and Honeyed Bananas on a lettuce-lined platter.

YIELD: 6 SERVINGS

Honeyed Bananas

6 bananas
Lemon juice

2 tablespoons butter
1/4 cup honey

Dip the bananas in lemon juice. Melt the butter in a skillet. Stir in the honey. Add the bananas. Cook over low heat for a few minutes or until hot and glazed, turning gently. Be careful not to overcook.

YIELD: 6 SERVINGS

Orange-Glazed Pork Chops

4 thick pork chops
Salt, pepper and paprika to taste
Vegetable oil
3 or 4 tablespoons water
5 tablespoons sugar
1 1/2 teaspoons cornstarch

1/4 teaspoon salt (optional)
1/4 teaspoon cinnamon
10 whole cloves
1/2 cup orange juice
4 orange slices

Season the pork chops with salt, pepper and paprika to taste. Brown in a small amount of oil in a skillet over high heat. Reduce the heat to low. Add the water. Cook, covered, for 45 to 60 minutes or until cooked through, turning occasionally to keep the pork chops moist. Combine the sugar, cornstarch, 1/4 teaspoon salt, cinnamon and cloves in a small saucepan. Add the orange juice and mix well. Cook until thickened and clear, stirring constantly. Add the orange slices and stir to coat. Pour over the pork chops and serve.

YIELD: 4 SERVINGS

A Log Smokehouse

An important building on the farmstead was the smokehouse. This building was usually built of logs chinked with mud. The smokehouse was used to keep the insects out, the meat cool in warm weather, and the meat from freezing in cold weather.

After the hog was killed, it was lowered into scalding water for exactly the correct number of minutes and the hair was scraped off. The hog was then hung on a scaffold and "dressed," placed on a platform (or table), and "blocked out" into conventional parts: hams, shoulders, middling (bacon or side meat), and other pieces. The meat was taken to the smokehouse to cool. After the meat had "cooled out," it was then thoroughly salted and placed in boxes or barrels to "take the salt." The meat was left buried in salt usually four to six weeks.

The salt was removed and the meat cleaned dry. It was then hung from the joists of the smokehouse. A fire was built inside the smokehouse directly on the dirt flour for "smoking" the meat. The fire was usually made with hickory wood and the thick pungent hickory fumes enveloped the hams and other pieces for two weeks. A "superior" ham was cured and cared for with patience and understanding.

Pork Chops with Saffron Rice

6 pork chops, cut $1/2$ to $3/4$ inch thick
$1/2$ teaspoon salt
$1/8$ teaspoon pepper
2 tablespoons shortening
1 (6-ounce) package saffron rice mix

$1/2$ cup chopped onion
1 beef bouillon cube
$13/4$ cups hot water
$1/2$ cup sour cream

Sprinkle the pork chops with the salt and pepper. Melt the shortening in a skillet. Add the pork chops. Cook until the pork chops are brown; drain. Add the rice mix and onion. Dissolve the bouillon cube in the hot water in a cup. Pour over the rice. Bring to a boil and reduce the heat. Cook, covered, over low heat for 40 minutes or until the pork chops are cooked through and the water is absorbed, stirring occasionally. Remove the pork chops; keep warm. Stir in the sour cream. Cook over low heat until heated through. Serve with the pork chops.

YIELD: 6 SERVINGS

Oven-Barbecued Pork Ribs

1 tablespoon vegetable oil
4 pounds country-style pork ribs
1 tablespoon vegetable oil
$1/2$ cup dry sherry
$1/2$ cup water
$1/2$ cup packed brown sugar
1 teaspoon salt
1 teaspoon celery seeds

1 teaspoon chili powder
$1/8$ teaspoon pepper
2 cups water
$1/4$ cup white vinegar
$1/4$ cup Worcestershire sauce
1 (12-ounce) bottle chili sauce
1 medium onion, chopped

Heat 1 tablespoon oil in a large nonstick skillet over medium-high heat until hot. Add $1/2$ of the ribs. Cook until the ribs are brown. Remove the ribs to a warm platter. Add 1 tablespoon oil to the skillet. Add the remaining ribs. Cook until the ribs are brown. Return the first batch of ribs to the skillet. Add the sherry and $1/2$ cup water. Bring to a boil and reduce the heat. Simmer, covered, for $11/2$ hours. Combine the brown sugar, salt, celery seeds, chili powder, pepper, 2 cups water, vinegar, Worcestershire sauce, chili sauce and onion in a 2-quart saucepan and mix well. Bring to a boil and reduce the heat to medium. Simmer, uncovered, for 1 hour. Remove the ribs to a 9×13-inch baking dish. Pour the sauce over the ribs. Bake, uncovered, at 300 degrees for 1 hour, basting occasionally.

YIELD: 4 SERVINGS

Marinated Pork Tenderloin

1/4 cup soy sauce
2 tablespoons chili sauce
2 tablespoons honey
1 tablespoon vegetable oil

1 green onion, minced
1 teaspoon curry powder
1 pork tenderloin

Combine the soy sauce, chili sauce, honey, oil, green onion and curry powder in a bowl and mix well. Place the pork in a large heavy sealable plastic bag. Pour the marinade over the top and seal the bag. Marinate in the refrigerator for 24 hours, turning occasionally. Arrange the pork on a rack in a roasting pan. Bake at 325 degrees for 1 1/2 hours or until the pork is cooked through.

YIELD: 8 SERVINGS

Baked Ham

1 (12- to 16-pound) fully cooked whole
　bone-in ham

1 tablespoon flour

Trim the rind and most of the fat from the ham. Add the flour to an oven baking bag and shake to coat. Place the ham in the prepared bag and secure with the nylon tie. Cut six 1/2-inch slits in the top of the bag. Place the bag in a large roasting pan, making sure the bag does not hang over the side. Bake at 350 degrees for 2 1/2 to 3 1/4 hours or until heated through.

YIELD: 20 TO 24 SERVINGS

Red-Eye Gravy

After frying slices of country ham in a skillet, drain the excess grease. Add a little water to the pan drippings, stirring with a metal spatula to deglaze the skillet. Add 1 tablespoon strong brewed coffee. Boil until of the desired consistency, stirring frequently. Serve with the sliced ham.

Old-Fashioned Sandwich Loaf

1 loaf Pepperidge Farm sandwich bread,
  cut into 16 slices
Egg Filling (below)
Ham Filling (page 49)

Mayonnaise
Thinly sliced tomatoes
Cream Cheese Topping (page 49)

Freeze the bread or let stand for 1 to 2 days before assembling the loaf. Trim the crusts from the bread. Bring the Egg Filling and Ham Filling to room temperature before assembling. Arrange 4 slices of the bread end to end on a serving board covered with foil. Spread the Egg Filling over the bread layer. Arrange 4 slices of bread over the filling end to end. Spread the top with mayonnaise and layer with tomatoes. Top with 4 bread slices end to end. Spread with the Ham Filling. Top with the remaining 4 slices of bread end to end. Spread the Cream Cheese Topping over the top and sides of the loaf to enclose the moisture content. Garnish with cuts of olives and pickles. Cover with waxed paper, inserting small flags in the top to keep the waxed paper from touching the top. Cover with foil. Chill in the refrigerator for 2 days. Remove from the refrigerator 1 hour before serving.

YIELD: 15 TO 20 SERVINGS

Egg Filling

4 hard-cooked eggs
2 green bell peppers, chopped
1/2 cup chopped walnuts

1/2 cup (1 stick) butter, softened
Lemon juice
Cayenne pepper to taste

Combine the eggs, bell peppers, walnuts, butter, lemon juice and cayenne pepper in a bowl and mix well. Force through an old-fashioned food grinder for the desired consistency. Store, covered, in the refrigerator for 24 hours before using.

YIELD: 2 CUPS

Ham Filling

1 1/3 cups ground ham
1/4 cup sweet pickle relish
2 teaspoons brown sugar

1/4 teaspoon ground cloves
Mayonnaise

Combine the ham, pickle relish, brown sugar and cloves in a bowl and mix well. Add enough mayonnaise to bind the mixture. Adjust the seasonings to taste. Force through an old-fashioned food grinder for the desired consistency. Store, covered, in the refrigerator for 24 hours before using.

YIELD: ABOUT 1 2/3 CUPS

Cream Cheese Topping

16 ounces cream cheese, softened
1/4 cup cream
2 tablespoons vinegar

1 teaspoon sugar
1/2 teaspoon salt

Combine the cream cheese, cream, vinegar, sugar and salt in a mixing bowl. Beat at high speed until smooth and fluffy.

YIELD: ABOUT 2 1/4 CUPS

History of the Sandwich Loaf

This sandwich loaf had been served throughout the entire twentieth century in the home of Charlotte Louise Hull Larned. Part of it comes from the earliest Fanny Farmer cookbook. The egg salad filling comes from the Home Economics department of Framingham Normal School, now Framingham College in Massachusetts. It was the first teachers' college in America. Dorothy Larned was dean of this school in the middle 1900s. This loaf must be made two days in advance. In the early days, it would sit in the pantry covered with moist towels and be about the correct temperature to be served. It was always the evening pickup meal on Thanksgiving, Christmas, and Easter.

1792

Kentucky became the fifteenth state.

The cornerstone for the White House was laid.

Twenty-four stockbrokers opened the New York Stock Exchange on Wall Street.

The Republican Party was formed. This party later became the Democratic Party.

The Bill of Rights went into effect.

Captain Gray entered the mouth of the Columbia River. This discovery was the basis for the United States claim to the Oregon region.

A treaty of peace was signed with the Wabash and Illinois Indians.

Brunch Soufflé

1 pound mild bulk pork sausage
6 eggs
2 cups milk or half-and-half
1 tablespoon dry mustard
1 teaspoon salt
6 slices white bread, trimmed, cubed
1 cup shredded mild Cheddar cheese

Brown the sausage in a skillet, stirring until crumbly; drain. Beat the eggs in a large bowl until fluffy. Add the milk, dry mustard, salt and bread cubes and mix well. Add the cheese and sausage and mix well. Spoon into an 8×12-inch glass baking dish. Chill, covered, for 8 to 12 hours. Bake, uncovered, at 350 degrees for 45 minutes or until set. Cut into squares to serve.

YIELD: 8 TO 10 SERVINGS

Note: You may also add sliced mushrooms or chopped onions.

Roast Ducks with Sausage Stuffing

2 ducks, dressed
2 ribs celery
1/2 apple
1/2 onion
1/4 teaspoon poultry seasoning

1/4 teaspoon thyme
Salt and seasoned pepper to taste
1 cup wine
Sausage Stuffing (below)

Arrange the ducks in a glass dish. Stuff each cavity with 1 rib celery, 1/4 apple, 1/4 onion, 1/8 teaspoon poultry seasoning and 1/8 teaspoon thyme. Rub the outside of the ducks with salt and seasoned pepper. Pour the wine over the ducks. Marinate, tightly covered, in the refrigerator for 8 to 12 hours. Drain the ducks, reserving the marinade. Remove the celery, apple and onion from the duck cavities and add to the reserved marinade. Stuff the Sausage Stuffing inside the cavities. Arrange in a baking pan. Pour the reserved marinade mixture over the ducks. Bake at 350 degrees until a meat thermometer inserted into the thickest portion registers 180 degrees, basting occasionally with the marinade.

YIELD: 4 SERVINGS

Sausage Stuffing

1 pound bulk pork sausage
2 (16-ounce) packages herb-seasoned
   stuffing mix

2 cups chopped celery
1 cup chopped onion
1 cup chopped pecans

Brown the sausage in a skillet, stirring until crumbly; drain. Prepare the stuffing mix using the package directions. Add the sausage, celery, onion and pecans and mix well.

YIELD: ENOUGH STUFFING FOR 2 DUCKS

Venison Stroganoff

1/2 cup minced onion
1/2 cup chopped celery
1/4 cup (1/2 stick) butter
1 1/2 pounds lean ground venison
2 tablespoons flour
2 teaspoons salt

1/4 teaspoon pepper
1 (8-ounce) can mushrooms, drained, or
    8 ounces fresh mushrooms
1 (10-ounce) can cream of chicken soup
1 cup sour cream

Sauté the onion and celery in the butter in a skillet until tender. Stir in the ground venison, flour, salt, pepper and mushrooms. Sauté for 5 minutes. Add the soup. Simmer, uncovered, for 20 minutes, adding water as needed for the desired consistency. Simmer, covered, for 20 minutes. Stir in the sour cream. Cook until heated through. Serve over rice, noodles, toast or hot potatoes.

YIELD: 4 TO 6 SERVINGS

Slow-Cooker Chicken Dressing

3 chicken leg quarters
3/4 cup chopped onion
3/4 cup chopped celery
1/4 cup (1/2 stick) margarine
8 cups corn bread crumbs
4 cups whole wheat bread crumbs

2 teaspoons salt
1/2 teaspoon pepper
1 teaspoon sage
6 cups chicken broth
1 (10-ounce) can cream of chicken soup
3 eggs, beaten

Place the chicken in a large stockpot. Cover with water. Bring to a boil. Boil until the chicken is cooked through; drain. Chop the chicken, discarding the skin and bones. Sauté the onion and celery in the margarine in a skillet until the onion is transparent. Combine the corn bread crumbs, whole wheat bread crumbs, salt, pepper and sage in a large bowl and toss to mix. Add the chicken broth, chicken soup and sautéed vegetables and mix well. Adjust the seasonings. Stir in the eggs and chopped chicken. Spoon into a slow cooker sprayed with nonstick cooking spray. Cook on High for 4 1/2 hours.

YIELD: 8 TO 10 SERVINGS

Note: You may spoon into a greased baking dish and bake at 350 degrees for 1 hour.

Chicken Casserole

1 (3-pound) whole chicken, cooked
2 cups cooked rice
1 cup chopped onion, sautéed
1 (10-ounce) can cream of chicken soup
1 (10-ounce) can cream of celery soup

1 (8-ounce) can sliced water chestnuts,
  drained
1 cup mayonnaise
1 cup crushed cornflakes

Chop the chicken, discarding the skin and bones. Combine the chicken, rice, sautéed onion, chicken soup, celery soup, water chestnuts and mayonnaise in a bowl and mix well. Spoon into a greased 2¹/2-quart baking dish. Sprinkle with the cornflake crumbs. Bake at 350 degrees for 30 minutes or until bubbly.

YIELD: 8 SERVINGS

Chicken Casserole with Almond Topping

2 cups chopped cooked chicken
2 cups chopped celery
2 cups cooked rice
1 (10-ounce) can cream of chicken soup
1¹/2 cups mayonnaise

1 tablespoon instant onion flakes
1 cup crushed cornflakes
¹/2 cup slivered almonds
2 tablespoons margarine, melted

Combine the chicken, celery, rice, soup, mayonnaise and onion in a bowl and mix well. Spoon into a greased 9×13-inch baking dish. Mix the cornflakes, almonds and melted margarine in a bowl. Sprinkle over the chicken mixture. Bake, uncovered, at 350 degrees for 30 minutes or until the top is light brown.

YIELD: 8 SERVINGS

Note: You may freeze the unbaked casserole and increase the baking time to 1 to 1¹/2 hours.

Fruited Chicken Salad

1¹/2 cups chopped cooked chicken
2 tablespoons thinly sliced celery
2 tablespoons chopped green bell pepper
1 green onion, chopped
2 teaspoons lemon juice
¹/2 cup seedless green grape halves
¹/2 cup mandarin oranges
3 tablespoons mayonnaise
2 tablespoons coarsely chopped pecans,
    toasted
¹/8 teaspoon salt
Dash of pepper

Combine the chicken, celery, bell pepper, green onion and lemon juice in a large bowl and toss to mix. Chill, covered, until ready to serve. Add the grapes, mandarin oranges, mayonnaise, pecans, salt and pepper and toss to mix well. Serve on lettuce-lined serving plates.

YIELD: 4 SERVINGS

1793

George Washington was inaugurated in his second term as president, with John Adams as his vice president.

Thomas Jefferson retired as secretary of state.

The first United States Mint was built in Philadelphia.

Eli Whitney applied for a patent on the cotton gin.

The Spanish Company was formed in St. Louis to explore the upper Missouri River and to establish the fur trade.

George Washington

Parmesan Chicken

1 cup bread crumbs	Salt and pepper to taste
1/3 cup grated Parmesan cheese	6 boneless chicken breasts
1 teaspoon garlic powder	1/2 cup (1 stick) butter, melted
1 tablespoon parsley	

Combine the bread crumbs, Parmesan cheese, garlic powder, parsley, salt and pepper in a bowl and mix well. Dip the chicken in the butter. Roll in the bread crumb mixture. Arrange in a 9×9-inch baking dish. Pour the remaining butter over the chicken. Bake, uncovered, at 350 degrees for 1 hour or until brown and cooked through.

YIELD: 4 TO 6 SERVINGS

Chicken Provençale

3 tablespoons olive oil	4 zucchini, sliced
4 large chicken breasts	4 ounces mushrooms, sliced
Salt and pepper to taste	2 tomatoes, chopped
1 garlic clove, chopped	1/2 cup chicken broth
1 onion, chopped	Salt and pepper to taste

Heat the olive oil in a nonstick skillet. Sprinkle the chicken with salt and pepper. Brown the chicken in the hot olive oil in the skillet. Add the garlic, onion, zucchini, mushrooms, tomatoes and chicken broth. Simmer for 25 to 30 minutes or until the chicken is cooked through, stirring occasionally. Season with salt and pepper.

YIELD: 4 SERVINGS

Old-Fashioned Chicken Pie

4 cups chopped cooked chicken
2 cups Sauce (below)
6 hard-cooked eggs, sliced
1/2 cup chopped celery

1 tablespoon grated onion
1 cup chicken broth
Pastry Strips (below)

Layer the chicken, Sauce, hard-cooked eggs, celery and onion 1/2 at a time in a greased 2-quart baking dish. Pour the broth over the top. Cover with the Pastry Strips to form a lattice. Bake at 375 degrees until heated through and the pastry is brown.

YIELD: 6 TO 8 SERVINGS

Sauce

1/4 cup (1/2 stick) butter or margarine

1/2 cup self-rising flour
2 1/2 cups chicken broth

Melt the butter in a medium saucepan. Stir in the self-rising flour. Add the chicken broth gradually, stirring constantly with a whisk until smooth. Cook over medium heat until the mixture boils and is thickened, stirring constantly. Remove from the heat.

YIELD: 6 TO 8 SERVINGS

Pastry Strips

2/3 cup shortening
1 cup self-rising flour

2/3 cup strained chicken broth

Cut the shortening into the self-rising flour in a bowl until crumbly. Add the broth gradually, stirring gently to form a dough. Roll into a rectangle on a lightly floured surface. Cut into strips.

YIELD: 6 TO 8 SERVINGS

Chicken Potpies

1 cup chopped onion
1 cup chopped celery
1 cup chopped carrots
6 tablespoons butter or margarine, melted
1 cup frozen tiny green peas
6 tablespoons flour
2 cups chicken broth
1 cup half-and-half
1 teaspoon salt
1/4 teaspoon pepper
4 cups chopped cooked chicken
*2 (17-ounce) packages frozen puff pastry,
    thawed*
1 egg yolk
1 tablespoon half-and-half

Sauté the onion, celery and carrots in the butter in a large skillet for
10 minutes. Stir in the peas and flour. Cook for 1 minute, stirring
constantly. Add the chicken broth and 1 cup half-and-half gradually.
Cook over medium heat until thickened and bubbly, stirring constantly.
Season with salt and pepper. Add the chicken and mix well. Ladle into
six 10-ounce ovenproof soup bowls, filling to within 3/4 inch of the rim.

Roll the pastry sheets 1/8 inch thick. Cut into 6 circles 1/2 inch larger
than the rim of the soup bowls. Cut the remaining pastry into
decorative shapes. Mix the egg yolk and 1 tablespoon half-and-half in a
bowl. Brush on one side of each circle. Arrange the circles brushed side
down over the bowls, folding the edges under and pressing to the sides
of the bowls. Arrange the decorative pastry shapes on the top. Brush
with the remaining egg mixture. Arrange the bowls on a large baking
sheet. Bake at 400 degrees for 15 to 20 minutes or until the tops are
puffed and brown.

YIELD: 6 SERVINGS

1794

John Jay concluded
a treaty of amity,
commerce, and
navigation with
the British.

James Monroe of
Virginia was named
United States minister
to France.

John Quincy Adams
was named United
States minister to The
Netherlands.

The first silver dollar was
coined in Philadelphia.

Eli Whitney was
granted a patent for
the cotton gin.

The United States Post
Office was established.

Main Dishes

Chicken Salad Pie

2 cups chopped cooked chicken
1 1/2 cups finely chopped celery
3 green onions with tops, chopped
1/2 cup shredded sharp Cheddar cheese
1/3 cup chopped pecans
1 1/2 cups mayonnaise

1 tablespoon lemon juice
1/4 teaspoon salt
1/2 teaspoon pepper
1 baked (9-inch) pie shell
1 cup crushed potato chips

Combine the chicken, celery, green onions, Cheddar cheese and pecans in a bowl and mix well. Mix the mayonnaise, lemon juice, salt and pepper in a bowl. Pour over the chicken mixture and mix well. Spoon into the baked pie shell. Sprinkle with the potato chips. Bake at 350 degrees for 25 minutes. Serve hot or cold.

YIELD: 8 SERVINGS

Note: You may use two 5-ounce cans water-pack chicken.

Chicken Spaghetti

3 large green bell peppers, chopped
4 large onions, chopped
1 stalk celery, chopped
3 cups chicken broth
1 (5- to 7-pound) hen, cooked
2 tablespoons chili powder
1 (16-ounce) package vermicelli

2 tablespoons salt
8 ounces sharp Cheddar cheese, shredded
1 (10-ounce) can cream of mushroom
  soup
1 (2-ounce) jar pimento
2 garlic cloves, minced
1 (6-ounce) can sliced mushrooms, drained

Cook the bell peppers, onions and celery in the chicken broth in a large saucepan until tender. Chop the hen, discarding the skin and bones. Add the hen and chili powder to the broth mixture. Cook for 15 minutes. Cook the pasta in boiling water seasoned with salt in a large saucepan for 10 minutes; drain. Rinse the pasta with cold water; drain. Add the pasta, Cheddar cheese, soup, pimento, garlic and mushrooms to the chicken mixture and toss to mix well. Spoon into 2 large greased baking dishes. Bake at 350 degrees for 45 minutes.

YIELD: 18 SERVINGS

Note: You may use two 3-pound chickens instead of the hen.

Chicken Stir-Fry

Olive oil
1 pound chicken breasts, cut into bite-size
  pieces
1 medium onion
1 red bell pepper, chopped
1 yellow bell pepper, chopped

1 (16-ounce) package small green beans
  (haricots verts), parboiled
1 large garlic clove, minced
1/2 teaspoon salt
1/4 to 1/2 teaspoon pepper
1/4 cup soy sauce

Spray a large skillet with nonstick cooking spray. Drizzle the skillet with olive oil. Heat until the skillet is hot. Add the chicken. Cook until light brown and cooked through. Remove the chicken to a platter and keep warm. Add the onion, bell peppers, green beans, garlic, salt, pepper and soy sauce to the skillet. Sauté until the vegetables are tender-crisp. Return the chicken to the skillet. Cook for 2 minutes longer.

YIELD: 2 SERVINGS

Turkey Divan

1 1/2 pounds fresh broccoli
1/4 cup grated Parmesan cheese
6 slices (or more) cooked turkey
1/4 cup (1/2 stick) butter
6 tablespoons flour
2 cups milk

1 1/2 teaspoons salt
1 teaspoon Worcestershire sauce
1 tablespoon lemon juice
1/2 cup whipping cream, whipped
1/4 cup grated Parmesan cheese

Trim the broccoli and cut into spears. Cook in a small amount of water in a saucepan for 5 minutes or until tender-crisp; drain. Arrange the broccoli in a buttered baking dish. Sprinkle with 1/4 cup Parmesan cheese. Arrange the turkey over the broccoli.

Melt the butter in a saucepan. Stir in the flour until smooth. Add the milk gradually. Cook until thickened, stirring constantly. Remove from the heat. Add the salt, Worcestershire sauce and lemon juice and mix well. Fold in the whipped cream. Pour over the turkey. Sprinkle with 1/4 cup Parmesan cheese. Bake at 400 degrees for 30 minutes.

YIELD: 4 SERVINGS

Baked Orange Roughy with Crab Meat Dressing

4 orange roughy fillets
Salt and pepper to taste
1/2 cup lemon juice
Lemon slices
Paprika to taste
Crab Meat Dressing (below)

Rinse the fish and pat dry. Sprinkle with salt and pepper. Arrange on a greased baking sheet. Pour the lemon juice over the fish. Arrange the lemon slices on top of the fish. Sprinkle with paprika. Bake at 400 degrees until the fish flakes easily. Arrange on serving plates. Top each with Crab Meat Dressing.

YIELD: 4 SERVINGS

Crab Meat Dressing

2 tablespoons butter
1/4 cup chopped green bell pepper
1/4 cup finely chopped celery
1 cup chopped mushrooms
1/4 cup finely chopped green onions
1 pound fresh lump crab meat
1/4 cup dry white wine

Melt the butter in a skillet. Add the bell pepper, celery, mushrooms and green onions. Sauté until tender. Add the crab meat and white wine. Cook until heated through, stirring occasionally. Remove from the heat and keep warm.

YIELD: 4 SERVINGS

1795

The first coin with the motto *E Pluribus Unum* was issued.

The United States signed a treaty with Spain establishing territorial boundaries and opening the Mississippi River.

A treaty of friendship, amity, and navigation was concluded with Spain.

A national arsenal was established at Harper's Ferry, West Virginia.

The first conveyor belt system was built in Pennsylvania.

Salmon with Lime Butter

1/4 cup (1/2 stick) unsalted butter,
  softened
3/4 teaspoon grated lime zest

1 pound salmon fillet
3 tablespoons olive oil
2 tablespoons minced green peppercorns

Mix the butter and lime zest in a small bowl. Chill, covered, until firm. Rub the fish with the olive oil. Press the peppercorns into the fish. Arrange on a grill rack. Grill over hot ashen coals for 4 to 5 minutes on each side or until the fish flakes easily. Serve on a heated platter with the lime butter. Garnish with lime wedges.

YIELD: 2 SERVINGS

Marinated Shrimp

2 pounds cooked shrimp, peeled
2 ribs celery, chopped
1 cup sliced red onions
1/2 (3-ounce) jar capers

1 teaspoon salt
2 dashes of Tabasco sauce
3/4 cup white vinegar
1/4 cup vegetable oil

Combine the shrimp, celery, red onions, undrained capers, salt and Tabasco sauce in a large bowl and toss to mix. Heat the vinegar and oil in a saucepan. Pour over the shrimp mixture and toss to coat. Marinate, covered, in the refrigerator for 24 hours or for up to 3 days before serving, tossing several times. Drain before serving.

YIELD: 12 SERVINGS

The First Important Cookbook

The first important cookbook written and published in the United States was Amelia Simmons' *American Cookery* in 1796. Ms. Simmons' recipes utilized native foods such as pumpkin, Indian meal (cornmeal), and maple syrup. Some innovative recipes included Indian puddings, watermelon rind pickles, and popular spruce beer. She suggested serving cranberry sauce with roast turkey and sang the praises of the Jerusalem artichoke. While endorsing the use of parsley, she shunned the use of "garlicks" and sage.

1796

Tennessee became the sixteenth state.

President Washington refused to run for a third term as president.

In his farewell address, President Washington urged the Republic to avoid permanent foreign alliances. Washington's mandate affected foreign policy throughout the next century.

The United States concluded a treaty of peace and friendship with Tripoli.

Andrew Jackson was elected to the House of Representatives.

The first elephant in America arrived in New York City.

The first pills were patented in the United States.

Gumbo

2 cups chopped celery
2 cups chopped green onions with tops
1/2 cup chopped bell pepper
1/4 cup (1/2 stick) butter
4 chicken bouillon cubes
2 cups hot water
9 tablespoons flour
1/2 cup (1 stick) butter
1 (14-ounce) can stewed tomatoes
1 cup tomato sauce
2 tablespoons Pickapeppa Sauce
1 bay leaf
2 garlic cloves, chopped
Seasoned salt to taste
1 (4-ounce) can crab claw meat
1 1/2 pounds frozen shrimp, peeled
1 (10-ounce) package frozen sliced okra
2 cups finely chopped parsley
Filé powder
Hot cooked rice

Sauté the celery, green onions and bell pepper in 1/4 cup butter in a heavy Dutch oven until tender. Dissolve the bouillon cubes in the hot water in a small bowl. Brown the flour in 1/2 cup butter in a skillet, stirring constantly. Add the bouillon. Cook until thickened, stirring constantly. Stir in the tomatoes and tomato sauce. Add the sautéed vegetables, Pickapeppa Sauce, bay leaf, garlic and seasoned salt. Stir in the undrained crab meat. Cook, covered, over low heat for 45 minutes, stirring frequently. Add the shrimp, okra and parsley. Cook, covered, for 15 minutes. Turn off the heat. Let stand, covered, for 1 hour or until ready to serve. Heat just before serving. Adjust the seasonings to taste. Discard the bay leaf. Sprinkle filé powder over the top. Ladle over hot cooked rice in individual serving bowls. Garnish with additional chopped parsley.

YIELD: 8 SERVINGS

Scalloped Oysters

1 pint oysters
2 cups medium-coarse cracker crumbs
1/2 cup (1 stick) butter, melted

3/4 cup light cream
1/4 teaspoon salt (optional)
1/4 teaspoon Worcestershire sauce

Drain the oysters, reserving 1/4 cup of the liquor. Mix the cracker crumbs with the melted butter in a bowl. Spread 1/3 of the buttered crumbs in an 8-inch round baking dish. Layer the oysters and remaining buttered crumbs 1/2 at a time in the prepared dish. Combine the cream, reserved oyster liquor, salt and Worcestershire sauce in a bowl and mix well. Pour over the layers. Bake at 350 degrees for 40 minutes.

YIELD: 4 SERVINGS

Oyster Stew

1 pint oysters
1/2 cup (1 stick) butter
1 cup light cream, heated
3 cups milk, scalded

1/2 teaspoon salt
1/2 teaspoon paprika
Pepper to taste

Heat the undrained oysters in the butter in a saucepan until the edges of the oysters curl. Add the heated cream and milk. Bring almost to a boil. Season with salt, paprika and pepper. Serve immediately.

YIELD: 4 SERVINGS

Note: You may thicken the stew with 1 to 2 tablespoons flour mixed with the melted butter before the liquid is added.

New England Clam Chowder

New England Clam Chowder is the hallmark of area cuisine. This recipe from Turner Fisheries of Boston has won so many "best chowder" prizes that it has been banned from future contests.

6 quahog clams, rinsed
1/2 cup water
10 cherrystone clams, rinsed
1/2 cup water
1 garlic clove, minced
1/2 cup (1 stick) clarified butter
1 medium onion, chopped
1 rib celery, chopped
1/2 teaspoon white pepper

1 small bay leaf
1/4 teaspoon thyme
1/2 cup (about) flour
5 cups clam juice
1 large potato, blanched, peeled,
   chopped
2 cups heavy cream
Salt and white pepper to taste

Place the quahog clams and 1/2 cup water in a saucepan and cover tightly. Steam until the clams open. Repeat the process with the cherrystone clams and 1/2 cup water. Drain the clams, reserving the broth. Remove the clams from the shells, discarding the shells. Chop the clams coarsely. Sauté the garlic in the clarified butter in a saucepan for 2 to 3 minutes. Add the onion, celery, 1/2 teaspoon white pepper, bay leaf and thyme. Sauté until the onion is transparent. Add enough flour to form a roux, stirring constantly. Cook over low heat for 5 minutes; do not brown. Add the clam juice and reserved broth gradually, stirring constantly to prevent lumps. Simmer for 10 minutes or until thickened, stirring frequently to prevent burning. Add the potato. Cook until tender. Stir in the cream and clams. Return to a boil. Season with salt and white pepper to taste. Discard the bay leaf before serving.

YIELD: 10 SERVINGS

Note: To clarify butter, melt the butter in a small saucepan over low heat until it foams. Remove from the heat and let stand until the milk solids settle to the bottom of the saucepan and the salt crystals settle on the top. Skim off the salt crystals and carefully pour the butter oil into a separate container, discarding the milk solids that have settled to the bottom.

Crab Cakes with Lime Sauce

5 slices firm white bread, crusts trimmed
1 cup milk
1 pound lump crab meat, picked
1/2 cup mayonnaise
1/3 cup finely chopped fresh cilantro leaves
1/3 cup finely chopped fresh dill
1/4 cup finely chopped fresh flat-leaf
   parsley

Juice of 1/2 lemon
1 small red onion, finely chopped
1/2 cup unbleached flour
2 eggs, beaten
3/4 cup dry bread crumbs
Salt and freshly ground pepper to taste
Vegetable oil for frying
Lime Sauce (below)

Soak the bread slices in the milk in a medium bowl for 5 to 10 minutes. Squeeze out
any excess milk. Crumble the bread back into the bowl. Add the crab meat, mayonnaise,
cilantro, dill, parsley, lemon juice, onion, flour, eggs and bread crumbs and mix well using
a wooden spoon. Season with salt and pepper. Chill, covered, for 30 minutes.

Shape the crab meat mixture into 4-inch patties. Arrange on a platter lined with paper
towels. Pour enough oil into a large heavy skillet to reach about a quarter of the way up
the side of the skillet. Heat the oil to 300 degrees. Add the patties. Fry until golden brown.
Remove to a platter lined with paper towels to drain. Serve with Lime Sauce.

YIELD: 6 SERVINGS

Lime Sauce

1/2 cup mayonnaise
1/4 cup sour cream

1 tablespoon lime juice
2 teaspoons grated lime zest

Combine the mayonnaise, sour cream, lime juice and lime zest in a bowl and mix well.
Chill, covered, until ready to serve.

YIELD: 6 SERVINGS

Staff of Life

THE ADAMS YEARS

1797–1800

1797

John Adams was
inaugurated as the
second president of
the United States.
Thomas Jefferson was
his vice president.

Congress levied a duty
on salt.

Congress declared all
treaties with France
annulled.

Andrew Jackson was
elected to the United
States Senate.

The secretary of
state reported that
300 United States
ships had been seized
at sea by France.

Sweet Potato Biscuits

1 egg, lightly beaten
1 cup mashed cooked sweet potatoes
1/4 to 1/2 cup sugar
2 tablespoons butter or margarine,
    softened
3 tablespoons shortening
2 cups (about) self-rising flour

Combine the egg, sweet potatoes, sugar, butter and shortening in a
mixing bowl and mix well. Stir in enough self-rising flour to form a
soft dough. The dough will be softer than regular bread dough. Knead
lightly on a floured surface a few times. Roll into a circle 1/3 inch thick.
Cut with a 2-inch biscuit cutter. Arrange on an ungreased baking sheet.
Bake at 350 degrees for 15 minutes or until golden brown.

YIELD: 1 1/2 DOZEN

Buttery Biscuit Rolls

1 cup (2 sticks) butter
1 cup sour cream
2 cups self-rising flour

Melt the butter in a large saucepan. Remove from the heat. Add the
sour cream and flour and mix well. Drop into ungreased miniature
muffin cups filling to the top. Bake at 350 degrees for 35 minutes.

YIELD: 2 DOZEN

Note: May be frozen. Do not use margarine in this recipe.

Bran Muffins

1 cup All-Bran
2 cups Bran Buds
1 cup boiling water
3 cups flour
2 1/4 teaspoons baking soda

1 teaspoon salt
1 1/4 cups sugar
1 cup plus 1 tablespoon shortening
2 eggs
2 cups buttermilk

Soak the All-Bran and Bran Buds in the boiling water in a bowl. Sift the flour, baking soda and salt together. Cream the sugar and shortening in a mixing bowl until light and fluffy. Add the eggs, buttermilk and cereal mixture and mix well. Add the flour mixture and mix to form a soft batter. Spoon into greased muffin cups filling about 2/3 full. Bake at 400 degrees for 15 to 20 minutes or until brown.

YIELD: 2 1/2 TO 3 DOZEN

John Adams

John Adams was vice president under George Washington. He gained prominence as a political thinker and writer. He helped edit Thomas Jefferson's Declaration of Independence and led the debate that ratified it in 1776. He chaired many important committees in Congress and represented his country in France and England both before and after the War of Independence. He was separated from his wife, Abigail, for long periods of time, as a result of his continuous service to his country. She and the children suffered many hardships because of his absences. His son, John Quincy Adams, who accompanied his father on several of his overseas assignments, later became president.

1798

Congress established the Navy Department. Benjamin Stoddert was appointed the first secretary of the Navy.

The patriotic song "Hail Columbia," which encouraged national support for the war with France, was written by Joseph Hopkinson.

Congress passed the Alien Act, which granted permission for the United States to deport dangerous aliens.

Congress approved an act creating the Mississippi Territory.

George Washington was appointed general of the United States Army in anticipation of war.

The United States began undeclared war with France.

Cranberry Coffee Cake

Although native to North America and Europe, most of the world's cranberry crop is harvested in Massachusetts. Cranberry bogs are both scenic and plentiful in the areas settled by Plymouth colonists. Native Americans enjoyed cranberries long before the white settlers came.

1/2 cup (1 stick) margarine, melted
1 cup sugar
2 eggs
1 cup sour cream
2 cups flour
1/4 teaspoon salt
1 teaspoon baking soda
1 teaspoon baking powder
1 tablespoon almond extract
1 (16-ounce) package frozen cranberries, thawed
1/2 cup chopped walnuts
1/2 cup confectioners' sugar
1 tablespoon warm water
1/2 teaspoon almond extract

Combine the margarine, sugar, eggs, sour cream, flour, salt, baking soda, baking powder, almond extract, cranberries and walnuts in the order listed in a large bowl, mixing well after each addition. Spoon into a greased and floured bundt pan. Bake at 350 degrees for 55 minutes. Cool in the pan for 20 minutes. Invert onto a serving plate. Beat the confectioners' sugar, warm water and almond extract in a small mixing bowl until smooth. Drizzle over the warm cake.

YIELD: 16 SERVINGS

Delicious Coffee Cake

1 1/2 cups sifted flour
1 tablespoon baking powder
1/4 teaspoon salt
3/4 cup sugar
1/4 cup shortening or margarine

1 egg
1/2 cup milk
1 teaspoon vanilla extract
Filling (below)

Sift the flour, baking powder, salt and sugar into a large bowl. Cut in the shortening until the mixture resembles cornmeal. Beat the egg and milk in a small bowl. Add to the flour mixture and blend well. Stir in the vanilla. Spread 1/2 of the batter into a greased and floured 8×8-inch baking pan. Sprinkle with 1/2 of the Filling. Spread with the remaining batter. Sprinkle with the remaining Filling. Bake at 375 degrees for 30 minutes.

YIELD: 16 SERVINGS

Filling

3/4 cup packed brown sugar
2 1/2 tablespoons flour
2 1/2 teaspoons cinnamon

2 1/2 tablespoons margarine, melted
1/4 cup chopped nuts

Mix the brown sugar, flour and cinnamon in a bowl. Add the margarine and stir to mix well. Stir in the nuts.

YIELD: 16 SERVINGS

The Staff of Life

1799

The United States frigate *Constellation*, under Commander Truxton, captured a French ship.

Congress voted to raise an army of 40,000 men.

James Monroe was elected governor of Virginia.

George Washington died at the age of 67 and was buried at Mount Vernon. President Adams asked all Americans to wear black crepe armbands for thirty days in memory of the former president.

Union "closed shop" rules, which required all employees to be and remain union members as a condition of employment, appeared in America.

Corn Bread

2 cups cornmeal
1 tablespoon baking powder
1 teaspoon salt
2 tablespoons sugar
1¹/2 cups milk
2 eggs, beaten
5 tablespoons shortening, melted

Sift the cornmeal, baking powder, salt and sugar into a bowl. Add the milk, eggs and shortening and mix well. Pour into a well-greased baking pan. Bake at 450 degrees for 20 minutes or until the corn bread tests done.

YIELD: 12 SERVINGS

Note: You may use 2 cups buttermilk instead of the milk, reducing the baking powder to 1 teaspoon and adding ¹/2 teaspoon baking soda.

Corn Pones

2 cups water-ground cornmeal
1 teaspoon salt
Lard the size of an egg
Boiling water

Combine the cornmeal and salt in a bowl. Cut in the lard until crumbly. Add enough boiling water to moisten the mixture sufficiently to mold. Shape by handfuls into pones, leaving the imprints of the fingers on the top. Arrange on a baking sheet. Bake at 350 degrees for about 30 minutes.

YIELD: 1 DOZEN

Snap Dragon Chew Bread

1 (16-ounce) package light brown sugar
1/2 cup (1 stick) margarine, softened
3 eggs, lightly beaten
2 cups self-rising flour

1 teaspoon vanilla extract
1/2 cup chopped nuts
1/2 cup raisins or chopped dates

Combine the brown sugar, margarine, eggs, self-rising flour and vanilla in a bowl and mix well. Stir in the nuts and raisins. Spoon into a greased 11×14-inch baking pan. Bake at 325 degrees for 30 minutes. Cut into squares while still warm.

YIELD: 24 SERVINGS

Williamsburg Sally Lunn

This bread was a mainstay in the households of Colonial Virginia and was also a favorite of James Monroe. It was always baked in a special Sally Lunn or Turk's-head mold.

1 cake yeast
1 cup warm milk
1/2 cup (1 stick) butter, softened

1/3 cup sugar
3 eggs, beaten
4 cups flour, sifted

Soak the cake of yeast in the warm milk in a bowl. Cream the butter and sugar in a large mixing bowl until light and fluffy. Add the eggs and beat well. Add the flour and yeast mixture alternately, beating well after each addition. Let rise in a warm place until doubled in bulk. Beat the dough well. Pour into a buttered Sally Lunn mold or 2 smaller molds. Let rise until doubled in bulk. Bake at 350 degrees for 50 minutes or until the loaf or loaves test done.

YIELD: 1 OR 2 LOAVES

Oat Bread

4 cups boiling water
2 cups rolled oats
1 envelope dry yeast
1/4 cup warm water

1 cup dark molasses
2 tablespoons salt
8 cups (or more) flour

Pour 4 cups boiling water over the oats in a large bowl. Let stand until cool. Dissolve the yeast in 1/4 cup warm water in a bowl. Add the molasses, salt and yeast mixture to the oat mixture and mix well. Add enough flour to form a stiff dough. Let rise in the bowl until doubled in bulk. Punch the dough down. Knead on a lightly floured surface until smooth and elastic. Divide into 3 portions. Shape each portion into a loaf. Arrange in 3 greased 5×7-inch loaf pans. Let rise until doubled in bulk. Bake at 400 degrees for 15 minutes. Reduce the oven temperature to 375 degrees. Bake for 30 to 40 minutes or until the loaves test done.

YIELD: 3 LOAVES

Pumpkin Bread

2/3 cup shortening
2 2/3 cups sugar
4 eggs
1 (16-ounce) can pumpkin
2/3 cup water

3 1/3 cups self-rising flour
1 teaspoon cinnamon
1 teaspoon ground cloves
1 1/3 cups chopped walnuts

Cream the shortening and sugar in a mixing bowl until light and fluffy. Add the eggs, pumpkin and water and mix well. Stir in the self-rising flour, cinnamon and cloves. Fold in the walnuts. Spoon into 2 greased 5×7-inch loaf pans. Bake at 350 degrees for 65 to 70 minutes or until the loaves test done.

YIELD: 2 LOAVES

Zucchini Bread

3 eggs
1 cup vegetable oil
2 cups sugar
1 tablespoon vanilla extract
2 cups grated peeled zucchini
1/2 cup chopped nuts

3 cups flour
1 teaspoon salt
1 teaspoon baking soda
1/4 teaspoon baking powder
1 teaspoon cinnamon
2 teaspoons almond extract

Process the eggs, oil, sugar, vanilla and zucchini in a blender until well blended. Add the nuts and pulse several times. Sift the flour, salt, baking soda, baking powder and cinnamon into a large bowl. Add the blended zucchini mixture and mix well. Pour into 2 greased and floured 5×7-inch loaf pans. Bake at 325 degrees for 1 hour or until the loaves test done.

YIELD: 2 LOAVES

Mom's Hot Rolls

This recipe has been passed down from generation to generation since 1866. The quantities of the ingredients are as close as can be "guestimated" from watching the rolls being prepared without the help of a recipe.

2 cups milk
2 tablespoons sugar
1 tablespoon salt
2 tablespoons (rounded) shortening

1 envelope dry yeast
1/4 cup warm water
5 to 6 cups flour

Combine the milk, sugar, salt and shortening in a small saucepan. Heat over low heat until scalded. Remove from the heat and cool to lukewarm. Dissolve the yeast in warm water in a small bowl. Combine the scalded milk mixture and yeast mixture in a large bowl. Add enough flour to form a stiff dough. Knead on a lightly floured surface until smooth and elastic. Place in a greased bowl and turn to coat the surface. Let rise until doubled in bulk. Punch the dough down. Let rise until doubled in bulk. Shape into rolls. Arrange in greased baking pans. Let rise until doubled in bulk. Bake at 350 degrees for 30 to 45 minutes or until golden brown.

YIELD: ABOUT 3 DOZEN

1800

Washington, DC
became the new capital
of the United States.

The second United
States census recorded a
population of 5,308,483
in 16 states.

President John Adams
reached a settlement
with France, ending the
undeclared naval war.

The Library of Congress
was established.

William Young became
the first shoemaker
in the United States
to make individual
shoes for the left and
right feet.

The first vaccination for
smallpox was given.

Mother's Refrigerator Rolls

$1/2$ cup shortening
$1/4$ cup sugar
1 teaspoon salt
$1/2$ cup water
1 envelope dry yeast
$1/2$ cup warm water
3 cups flour
1 egg, beaten
Melted butter

Combine the shortening, sugar, salt and $1/2$ cup water in a saucepan.
Bring to a boil and remove from the heat. Let stand until cool. Dissolve
the yeast in $1/2$ cup warm water in a bowl. Combine the shortening
mixture and yeast mixture in a large mixing bowl. Add the flour and
egg. Beat at medium speed for 1 minute. Place in a greased bowl and
turn to coat the surface. Chill, covered, for 8 to 12 hours.

Turn onto a lightly floured surface and knead lightly. Kneading too
long will make the rolls tough. Roll the dough into a circle. Cut into
circles and dip in melted butter. Arrange in baking pans. Let rise for 45
minutes to 2 hours or until doubled in bulk. Bake at 400 degrees for
5 minutes or until light brown.

YIELD: 1 $1/2$ DOZEN

Auntie's Refrigerator Potato Rolls

1 cup milk, scalded
2/3 cup shortening
1/3 cup sugar
2 envelopes dry yeast
1/2 cup warm water

6 cups flour
1 teaspoon salt
2 eggs
1 cup finely mashed unseasoned potatoes
Melted butter

Pour the scalded milk over the shortening and sugar in a large mixing bowl. Let stand until cooled to lukewarm. Dissolve the yeast in the warm water in a small bowl. Sift the flour and salt together. Add the eggs and potatoes to the lukewarm milk mixture and mix well. Stir in the yeast mixture. Add the flour mixture a small amount at a time to form a stiff dough, mixing well after each addition. Knead on a lightly floured surface until smooth and elastic. Divide the dough into 2 portions. Place each portion in a greased medium bowl, turning to coat the surface. Chill, covered, for 5 to 12 hours. Pinch off 1/3 of the dough at a time and roll into a circle 1/3 inch thick. Cut into circles and dip in melted butter. Arrange in baking pans. Let rise for 2 hours or until doubled in bulk. Bake at 400 degrees for 5 minutes or until light golden brown.

YIELD: 3 DOZEN

John Adams

The Staff of Life

Orange Rolls

2 envelopes dry yeast
1/4 cup warm (105 to 115 degrees) water
3 cups flour
1 cup sugar
1 teaspoon salt
2 eggs
1/2 cup (1 stick) butter or margarine,
   melted

2/3 cup warm (105 to 115 degrees) water
1 (5-ounce) can evaporated milk (2/3 cup)
2 to 3 cups flour
Melted butter or margarine
1 cup flaked coconut, toasted
3/4 cup sugar
1 1/2 tablespoons grated orange zest
Orange Glaze (below)

Dissolve the yeast in 1/4 cup warm water in a large mixing bowl. Let stand for 5 minutes. Add 3 cups flour, 1 cup sugar, salt, eggs, 1/2 cup butter, 2/3 cup warm water and evaporated milk. Beat at low speed until smooth. Add enough of the remaining 2 to 3 cups flour gradually to form a soft dough. Place the dough in a well-greased bowl and turn to coat the surface. Let rise, covered, in a warm place for 1 hour. Punch the dough down. Knead on a lightly floured surface 4 or 5 times. Divide the dough into 6 portions. Roll 1 portion into an 8-inch circle. Brush with melted butter. Combine the coconut, 3/4 cup sugar and orange zest in a bowl. Sprinkle 1/6 of the mixture over the dough. Cut the circle into 8 wedges. Roll each wedge up tightly beginning at the wide end and seal the points. Arrange point side down on a greased baking sheet, curving into a half-moon shape. Repeat with the remaining dough and coconut mixture.

Let rise, covered, in a warm place for 1 hour or until doubled in bulk. Bake at 325 degrees for 15 minutes or until light brown. Pour the Orange Glaze over the warm rolls.

YIELD: 4 DOZEN

Orange Glaze

1/4 cup (1/2 stick) butter or margarine,
   melted
1/2 cup sour cream

2 tablespoons orange juice
3 to 3 1/2 cups sifted confectioners' sugar

Combine the butter, sour cream and orange juice in a bowl and mix well. Stir in enough of the confectioners' sugar to make of a glaze consistency.

YIELD: 2 CUPS

Old-Fashioned Rusk or Sweet Rolls

2 cups milk, scalded
2 tablespoons sugar
1 envelope dry yeast
3¹/4 cups flour
²/3 cup sugar

¹/2 cup shortening
2 eggs
3³/4 cups flour
1 teaspoon salt

Combine the scalded milk and 2 tablespoons sugar in a large bowl and mix well. Cool slightly. Add the yeast and stir until dissolved. Add 3¹/4 cups flour and mix well. Let rise, covered, for 1 hour. Beat ²/3 cup sugar, shortening and eggs in a mixing bowl until light and fluffy. Add to the flour mixture and mix well. Add 3³/4 cups flour and 1 teaspoon salt and mix to form a soft dough. Let rise, covered, until doubled in bulk. Knead on a lightly floured surface. Shape into buns a little larger than the size of an egg. Arrange on a baking sheet. Let rise, covered, until doubled in bulk. Bake at 375 degrees for 20 minutes. Remove from the oven and top with your favorite plain frosting, if desired.

YIELD: 3¹/2 DOZEN

Soda Crackers

4 cups flour
1 teaspoon salt
¹/2 teaspoon baking soda

1 cup (2 sticks) butter
³/4 cup sour milk or buttermilk

Sift the flour, salt and baking soda into a large bowl. Cut in the butter until crumbly. Add the sour milk, stirring to form a stiff dough. Roll and turn repeatedly on a lightly floured surface until the dough is very stiff. Roll into a very thin rectangle. Cut into squares. Prick with a fork. Arrange on a baking sheet. Bake at 400 degrees until the edges are light brown.

YIELD: 50 TO 60 CRACKERS

Heritage Side Dishes

THE JEFFERSON YEARS

1801–1808

1801

Thomas Jefferson was inaugurated as the third president of the United States. Aaron Burr was his vice president. Jefferson and Burr had tied on electoral votes so the vote went to the House of Representatives, which elected Jefferson.

President Jefferson became the first president to be inaugurated in Washington, DC.

James Madison became secretary of state. His wife, Dolley Payne Madison, became a great social leader in Washington.

President Jefferson published the first parliamentary rules of order.

Tripoli declared war on the United States.

At receptions given by President Jefferson, guests shook hands with the president rather than bowing.

Asparagus and Peas Casserole

1 (15-ounce) can asparagus, drained
2 hard-cooked eggs, chopped
2 tablespoons shredded cheese
1 (16-ounce) can green peas, drained
1/4 cup (1/2 stick) butter
1/2 teaspoon salt
1/4 teaspoon pepper
1 (10-ounce) can cream of mushroom soup
1/2 cup milk
Cracker crumbs
1/3 cup almonds, toasted
1/4 teaspoon paprika

Layer the asparagus, hard-cooked eggs, cheese and green peas in a buttered baking dish. Dot with some of the butter. Season with the salt and pepper. Mix the soup and milk in a small bowl. Pour over the layers. Sprinkle with cracker crumbs and toasted almonds. Dot with the remaining butter. Sprinkle with the paprika. Bake at 350 degrees for 30 minutes.

YIELD: 10 SERVINGS

Cold Asparagus with Pecans

1¹/2 pounds fresh young asparagus, or
   2 (10-ounce) packages frozen asparagus
³/4 cup finely chopped pecans
2 tablespoons vegetable oil

¹/4 cup cider vinegar
¹/4 cup soy sauce
¹/4 cup sugar
Pepper to taste

Cook the asparagus in boiling water to cover in a saucepan for 6 to 7 minutes or until tender and bright green; drain. Rinse under cold water; drain. Arrange in 1 or 2 layers in an oblong serving dish. Combine the pecans, oil, cider vinegar, soy sauce and sugar in a bowl and mix well. Pour over the asparagus, lifting the asparagus so the mixture penetrates to the bottom. Sprinkle with pepper. Marinate, covered, in the refrigerator for up to 36 hours before serving.

YIELD: 6 TO 8 SERVINGS

Thomas Jefferson

Thomas Jefferson, a Virginian by birth, studied law with the state's leading legal scholar, George Wythe, after his graduation from William and Mary. He designed and built his home, Monticello, and was elected to Virginia's House of Burgesses.

In the year leading up to the revolution, Jefferson was prominent in his growing opposition to the British Parliament's taxation policies and Britain's general control over the colonies. He was named to a five-person committee, which included John Adams and Benjamin Franklin, to draft a formal statement of the reasons for the colonies' impending break with Britain. He wrote the first draft of the document that would become the Declaration of Independence. He later became governor of Virginia.

As the Revolutionary War drew to a close, he was called to serve as a delegate to the Continental Congress and later succeeded Benjamin Franklin as American minister to France. He was much enamoured with French cuisine. His endless experimentation in animal and plant husbandry as well as food preparation; and his Herculean accomplishment as a host, over his lifetime, of thousands in his home, qualify him for the title, "Father of His Country's Cuisine."

Asparagus Dijon

1/3 cup mayonnaise
1 1/2 teaspoons Dijon mustard

Dash of garlic powder or onion powder
1 (12-ounce) can whole asparagus spears

Combine the mayonnaise, Dijon mustard and garlic powder in a bowl and mix well. Heat the asparagus in a saucepan over medium heat; drain. Arrange in a serving bowl. Spoon or pipe the mayonnaise mixture over the asparagus. Garnish with chopped herbs.

YIELD: 2 OR 3 SERVINGS

Barbecued Mixed Beans

1/2 cup minced onion
2 garlic cloves, minced
1/4 cup minced green bell pepper
1/3 cup butter or margarine
2 teaspoons brown sugar
1 teaspoon dry mustard

2 (20-ounce) cans kidney beans, drained
1 (20-ounce) can lima beans, drained
1 (30-ounce) can pork and beans
1/4 cup ketchup
2 tablespoons vinegar
Salt and pepper to taste

Sauté the onion, garlic and bell pepper in the butter in a large skillet. Stir in the brown sugar, dry mustard, kidney beans, lima beans, pork and beans, ketchup and vinegar and mix well. Season with salt and pepper. Pour into a 2-quart baking dish. Bake, covered, at 350 degrees for 25 minutes.

YIELD: 8 SERVINGS

Lima Bean Casserole

2 (10-ounce) packages frozen baby
  lima beans
2 slices bacon, chopped
1 medium onion, minced
1 garlic clove, crushed
1 (10-ounce) can cream of
  mushroom soup
1/2 cup sour cream
2 tablespoons dry sherry
1 (3-ounce) can French-fried onions,
  lightly crushed

Cook the lima beans in a saucepan using the package directions just until tender; drain. Fry the bacon in a skillet until crisp. Remove the bacon with a slotted spoon to paper towels to drain. Add the onion and garlic to the drippings in the skillet. Sauté until tender. Mix the soup, sour cream and wine in a bowl until smooth. Add to the skillet. Heat just to the boiling point. Stir in the lima beans and bacon. Spoon into a 1 1/2-quart baking dish. Sprinkle with the French-fried onions. Bake at 325 degrees for 25 minutes or until hot and bubbly.

YIELD: 8 SERVINGS

Note: You may substitute one 10-ounce package whole kernel corn for one of the packages of lima beans and add 2 or 3 tablespoons chopped pimentos for color.

1802

The United States Military Academy at West Point, New York, opened on July 4.

The war with Tripoli was recognized by Congress.

James Monroe was appointed Minister Envoy Extraordinary to France.

John Quincy Adams became a state senator in Massachusetts.

The United States entered its fourth economic depression since 1790, this one lasting until 1805.

The United States Corps of Engineers was established.

Boundaries were prescribed for Ohio as the first step toward statehood.

Heritage Side Dishes

Sugar and Spice Beets

2 tablespoons butter or margarine
2 tablespoons sugar
1 teaspoon lemon juice

1/4 teaspoon cinnamon
Dash of ground ginger
1 (8-ounce) can beets

Combine the butter, sugar, lemon juice, cinnamon and ginger in a small saucepan. Heat just to the boiling point. Add the beets, stirring to coat. Heat to serving temperature.

YIELD: 2 SERVINGS

Broccoli and Rice Casserole

This recipe is over forty years old and is a perfect side dish for ham or turkey.

2 (10-ounce) packages frozen chopped
   broccoli
1 cup instant rice, cooked
1 small onion, chopped

1/2 cup milk
1 (10-ounce) can cream of chicken soup
1/2 cup Cheez Whiz
2 tablespoons butter, melted

Cook the broccoli in a saucepan using the package directions; drain. Combine the broccoli, cooked rice and onion in a large bowl. Mix the milk, soup, Cheez Whiz and butter in a small bowl until smooth. Add to the broccoli mixture and mix well. Spoon into a baking dish. Bake at 350 degrees for 35 minutes.

YIELD: 8 SERVINGS

Company Broccoli Casserole

2 (10-ounce) packages frozen
    broccoli florets
1 (10-ounce) can cream of shrimp soup
1 tablespoon lemon juice
1 (8-ounce) package soft whipped cream
    cheese with chives, or 1 (8-ounce) log
    garlic cheese
1/2 cup slivered almonds

Cook the broccoli in a saucepan using the package directions; drain.
Arrange in a 2-quart baking dish. Heat the soup in a saucepan. Add
the lemon juice and soft whipped cream cheese and mix until smooth.
Pour over the broccoli. Sprinkle with the almonds. Bake at 350 degrees
until bubbly.

YIELD: 6 SERVINGS

*Note: You may use herbed bread crumbs dotted with butter instead of the
slivered almonds.*

1803

Ohio became the
seventeenth state.

The United States
purchased the Louisiana
Territory from France
for eighty million francs
(fifteen million dollars),
which amounted to four
cents per acre.

A treaty with France was
ratified by Congress.

Governor Claiborne of
the Mississippi Territory
took possession of the
Louisiana Territory for
the United States.

Governor Harrison
negotiated a treaty
with the Indians at
Fort Wayne (in what
is now Indiana).

Thomas Moore invented
the refrigerator in
Baltimore, Maryland.

J. J. Audubon of
Pennsylvania began
banding and tagging
birds for study.

Connecticut Corn Pudding

2 slices bacon
1/2 cup chopped green bell pepper
1 small onion, chopped
2 cups fresh whole kernel corn
1/2 cup soft bread crumbs

2 cups milk
2 eggs, beaten
Salt and pepper to taste
1/2 cup buttered bread crumbs

Fry the bacon in a skillet until crisp. Drain the bacon, reserving 2 tablespoons bacon drippings in the skillet. Crumble the bacon into a small bowl. Sauté the bell pepper and onion in the reserved drippings in the skillet until the onion is transparent. Add the corn, 1/2 cup soft bread crumbs, milk, eggs and crumbled bacon and mix well. Season with salt and pepper. Spoon into a greased 11/2-quart baking dish. Sprinkle with 1/2 cup buttered bread crumbs. Bake at 375 degrees for 40 minutes.

YIELD: 6 SERVINGS

Corn Pudding

1 (17-ounce) can cream-style corn
2 eggs, lightly beaten
2 tablespoons flour
2 tablespoons sugar
1 cup evaporated milk

1/4 cup (1/2 stick) butter or margarine, melted
Salt and white pepper to taste
Paprika

Combine the corn, eggs, flour, sugar, evaporated milk, butter, salt and white pepper in a bowl and mix well. Spoon into a buttered shallow baking dish. Sprinkle with paprika. Bake at 300 degrees for 1 hour.

YIELD: 4 SERVINGS

Eggplant and Tomato Bake

6 slices bacon, chopped
1/2 green bell pepper, chopped
1 small or medium onion, chopped
4 medium tomatoes, peeled, chopped
1 medium or large eggplant, peeled,
   chopped

Salt and pepper to taste
2 slices Cheddar cheese
1/4 to 1/2 cup bread crumbs

Fry the bacon in a skillet until crisp. Remove the bacon to paper towels to drain. Crumble the bacon. Drain the skillet, reserving 2 tablespoons of the drippings in the skillet. Add the bell pepper and onion. Sauté until soft. Add the tomatoes and eggplant. Cook for 8 to 10 minutes. Season with salt and pepper. Spoon into a buttered baking dish. Layer the cheese over the top. Sprinkle with the bread crumbs and the crumbled bacon. Bake at 350 degrees for 25 to 30 minutes or until bubbly.

YIELD: 6 TO 8 SERVINGS

Swiss Green Beans

2 slices Swiss cheese
1 (16-ounce) can French green beans,
   drained

1/2 cup sour cream
2 tablespoons chopped onion
1 tablespoon flour

Cut 1 slice of the Swiss cheese into bite-size pieces. Cut the remaining slice of Swiss cheese into strips. Combine the green beans, sour cream, onion and flour in a bowl and mix well. Stir in the bite-size pieces of Swiss cheese. Spoon into a baking dish. Arrange the Swiss cheese strips over the top. Bake at 350 degrees for 25 minutes or until the Swiss cheese melts.

YIELD: 4 TO 6 SERVINGS

Hoppin' John

This is a favorite side dish to serve on New Year's Day.

3 or 4 slices bacon
1 cup uncooked rice
1/2 cup water
1 1/2 cups tomato juice
1 (5-ounce) jar pimento cheese spread
1 medium onion, chopped
1 teaspoon salt

1 teaspoon celery salt (optional)
1 tablespoon Worcestershire sauce
1/4 teaspoon Tabasco Sauce
1 (15-ounce) can black-eyed peas
Chopped fresh parsley to taste
1 (2-ounce) jar chopped pimento, drained

Cook the bacon in a large skillet until crisp. Remove the bacon to paper towels to drain. Crumble the bacon. Add the rice, water, tomato juice, pimento cheese spread, onion, salt, celery salt, Worcestershire sauce and Tabasco sauce to the bacon drippings in the skillet and mix well. Spoon into a buttered 2-quart baking dish. Bake, tightly covered, for 1 1/2 hours. Add the black-eyed peas and toss lightly to mix. Bake, covered, for 30 minutes. Sprinkle with the crumbled bacon, parsley and pimento just before serving.

YIELD: 6 SERVINGS

Thomas Jefferson and the Enlargement of Gastronomical Boundaries

When President Jefferson signed the Louisiana Purchase in 1803, he did more than enlarge the territorial boundaries of the United States. He enlarged the gastronomical boundaries as well. New Orleans and the whole southern Mississippi River area offered a range of cooking unknown to Colonial America. Due to French and African influences and decades of trading with exotic ports, these areas produced spices, scents, and commodities unknown in the South and East. Products such as garlic, hot Creole mustard, thyme, shallots, saffron, and rice (served as a main course or dessert) were new sensations to many in the United States. A great Louisiana favorite was gumbo, a thick soup or stew of meat or fish, corn, tomatoes, and okra. A similar recipe to ours (page 62) was found in one of his old cookbooks.

Vidalia Onion Casserole

This looks and tastes like French onion soup.

> 6 Vidalia onions
> 6 tablespoons butter
> 16 ounces Swiss cheese, shredded
> 1 (10-ounce) can cream of chicken soup
> 1 cup half-and-half
> 2 tablespoons soy sauce
> 1 miniature loaf French bread
> Butter

Cut the onions into 1/4-inch slices. Sauté the onions in 6 tablespoons butter in a large skillet until transparent. Arrange in a 9×13-inch baking dish. Cover with the Swiss cheese. Mix the soup, half-and-half and soy sauce in a small bowl. Pour over the Swiss cheese. Cut the French bread into thick slices. Spread each slice with butter. Arrange over the sauce. Bake at 350 degrees for 30 minutes.

YIELD: 6 TO 8 SERVINGS

Thomas Jefferson

1804

The upper Louisiana District was formally transferred to the United States by France.

Andrew Jackson and his wife built their estate, the Hermitage, in the Tennessee wilderness.

Lewis and Clark traveled to North Dakota, where they established their winter camp near what is now Bismarck.

Stephen Decatur became a national hero for recapturing the *Philadelphia* in Tripoli.

Alexander Hamilton was fatally wounded in a pistol duel with Vice President Aaron Burr.

Modern printer's ink was brought into use by J. Johnston in Philadelphia.

Bananas were imported to the United States for the first time.

Danish Potato Salad

4 cups cooked cubed potatoes
1 (10-ounce) package frozen green peas
1 pint grape tomatoes

1 (4-ounce) can sliced black olives,
  drained
Dill Bleu Cheese Dressing (below)

Combine the potatoes, green peas, tomatoes and olives in a bowl and toss to mix. Add the Dill Bleu Cheese Dressing and toss to mix well. Chill, covered, in the refrigerator for 24 hours before serving.

YIELD: 8 SERVINGS

Note: You may store in the refrigerator for several days.

Dill Bleu Cheese Dressing

1 1/2 cups sour cream
1/4 cup lemon juice
1 teaspoon grated onion
1 teaspoon dillweed

1 teaspoon salt
1/8 teaspoon pepper
Pinch of sugar
8 ounces Danish bleu cheese, crumbled

Combine the sour cream, lemon juice, onion, dillweed, salt, pepper and sugar in a bowl and mix well. Stir in the bleu cheese. Store, covered, in the refrigerator.

YIELD: ABOUT 2 CUPS

German Potato Salad

This is an old family recipe. When we were children, we had a cleaning lady who was a fabulous cook. Mom was making this one day and Bertha was watching her as she cleaned. Finally she went over to Mom and announced, "Add pepper! You have to see the pepper!" She was right. It tastes much better that way.

1 package new potatoes	¹/3 cup flour
8 to 12 ounces bacon, cut into thick slices, chopped	¹/4 cup (¹/2 stick) butter
	¹/2 cup vinegar
2 cups water	3 medium onions, coarsely chopped
³/4 cup sugar	Salt and pepper to taste

Scrub the potatoes. Boil the potatoes in water to cover in a saucepan until almost tender; drain. Fry the bacon in a large deep frying pan until crisp. Remove the bacon to paper towels to drain, reserving the bacon drippings in the pan. Stir the water, sugar, flour, butter and vinegar into the reserved bacon drippings. Cook over medium heat until thickened, stirring constantly.

Peel the potatoes and cut into slices. Layer the potatoes, onions, bacon, salt and pepper in a small roasting pan. Pour the hot mixture over the layers and stir. Add more pepper if you can't see it. Bake at 350 degrees for 45 minutes. Serve hot.

YIELD: 18 SERVINGS

Note: This recipe reheats well in the microwave or it can be frozen.

Heritage Side Dishes

1805

Thomas Jefferson was inaugurated for his second term. George Clinton was inaugurated vice president.

At Derma, Tripoli, the United States flag was raised for the first time over a fort in Europe.

A Treaty of Peace and Amity was concluded between the United States and Tripoli.

Disagreements began with Great Britain, which would lead eventually to the War of 1812.

Congress adopted President Jefferson's plan to negotiate the purchase of Florida.

The city of Detroit was destroyed by fire.

Lewis and Clark reached the Pacific Ocean at the mouth of the Columbia River.

Robert Fulton built the first marine torpedo.

Squash Soufflé

2 cups chopped drained parboiled
    yellow squash
1 tablespoon grated onion
1/2 teaspoon salt
Pepper to taste
2 egg yolks
2 tablespoons butter
1 1/2 tablespoons flour
1 cup milk
2 egg whites, stiffly beaten

Combine the squash, onion, salt and pepper in a large bowl and mix well. Add the egg yolks and mix well. Melt the butter in a saucepan. Stir in the flour. Add the milk gradually, stirring constantly. Cook until thickened, stirring constantly. Remove from the heat. Fold the stiffly beaten egg whites into the squash mixture. Stir in the sauce. Spoon into a greased baking dish. Bake at 275 degrees for 30 minutes or until set.

YIELD: 4 SERVINGS

Squash Dressing

6 yellow squash, chopped
1/2 Vidalia onion, chopped
1 egg
2 tablespoons butter, melted
1 envelope Mexican corn bread mix
1 (8-ounce) can cream-style corn
1/4 cup picante sauce

Cook the squash and onion in enough water to cover in a saucepan until soft; drain. Add the egg, butter, corn bread mix, corn and picante sauce and mix well. Spoon into a 2-quart greased baking dish. Bake at 350 degrees for 50 minutes.

YIELD: 8 SERVINGS

Stuffed Squash

8 medium yellow squash
2 slices bacon, chopped
1/2 cup chopped onion
1/2 cup chopped green bell pepper

1/2 cup cracker crumbs
1 egg, lightly beaten
Salt and pepper to taste
1 cup shredded Cheddar cheese

Rinse the squash and pat dry. Arrange the squash in a microwave-safe dish. Pierce the top of the squash with a fork. Cover loosely with plastic wrap. Microwave on High until soft to the touch. Let stand until cool. Cut off the stem ends. Lay each squash horizontally on a clean surface and cut off a slice 1/2 inch thick from the top. Chop the slices of squash in a bowl. Scoop the pulp from the squash into the bowl, leaving the shells intact. Chop the pulp.

Fry the bacon in a skillet until crisp. Remove the bacon to paper towels to drain, reserving the drippings in the skillet. Add the onion and bell pepper to the reserved bacon drippings. Sauté until tender. Stir in the chopped squash and cracker crumbs. Remove from the heat. Add the egg, salt and pepper and mix well. Stuff into the squash shells. Arrange in a greased 9×13-inch baking dish. Bake at 350 degrees for 25 minutes. Sprinkle with the Cheddar cheese and bacon. Bake for 5 minutes or until the cheese melts and is just beginning to brown.

YIELD: 8 SERVINGS

Note: You may use cheese cracker crumbs instead of plain cracker crumbs.

Autumn Pudding

3 cups mashed cooked sweet potatoes
1 cup sugar
1/2 teaspoon salt
2 eggs, beaten
1/4 cup (1/2 stick) butter
1/2 cup milk

1 tablespoon vanilla extract
1 cup packed brown sugar
1/3 cup flour
1 cup coarsely chopped pecans
1/4 cup (1/2 stick) butter, softened

Combine the sweet potatoes, sugar, salt, eggs, 1/4 cup butter, milk and vanilla in a bowl and mix well. Spoon into a 2 1/2-quart baking dish. Combine the brown sugar, flour, pecans and 1/4 cup butter in a bowl and mix well. Spread over the sweet potato mixture. Bake at 350 degrees for 30 minutes.

YIELD: 6 TO 8 SERVINGS

Roasted Sweet Potato Wedges

5 pounds sweet potatoes, peeled, cut
   crosswise into halves
2 tablespoons olive oil
1 teaspoon salt

1/2 teaspoon coarsely ground pepper
2/3 cup peach preserves
1/2 teaspoon cinnamon

Combine the sweet potatoes, olive oil, salt and pepper in a large bowl and toss to coat. Arrange the sweet potatoes in a single layer on 2 baking sheets. Roast at 450 degrees on 2 oven racks for 30 to 40 minutes or until tender. Combine the peach preserves and cinnamon in a small bowl and beat with a wire whisk until blended. Spread evenly over the sweet potatoes. Roast for 5 minutes longer or until the glaze is hot and bubbly.

YIELD: 14 SERVINGS

Thomas Jefferson

Thomas Jefferson was never a great eater, but what he did eat he wanted to be very choice. He enjoyed simple fare with an emphasis on vegetables. He was extremely fond of salads, and wanted to produce olive oil in this country. As a substitute for olive trees, he experimented with sesame (benne) seeds, which can be crushed to make oil.

Marinated Tomatoes

3 tomatoes
1/3 cup olive oil
1/4 cup red wine vinegar
1 teaspoon salt

1/2 teaspoon pepper
2 tablespoons chopped onion
1/2 garlic clove, crushed
1 teaspoon chopped parsley

Cut the tomatoes into slices 1/2 inch thick. Arrange in a shallow dish. Combine the olive oil, red wine vinegar, salt, pepper, onion, garlic and parsley in a jar with a tight-fitting lid. Secure the lid and shake to mix well. Pour over the tomatoes. Marinate, covered, in the refrigerator for several hours before serving.

YIELD: 6 SERVINGS

Tomato Pie

1 (10-inch) deep-dish pie shell
3 or 4 ripe tomatoes, cut into slices
    1/2 inch thick
2 tablespoons chopped fresh basil
1/2 teaspoon salt

1/4 teaspoon pepper
8 ounces mozzarella cheese, shredded
8 ounces Parmesan cheese, shredded
1 cup light mayonnaise

Bake the pie shell at 350 degrees until light brown. Arrange the tomato slices in the partially baked pie shell. Sprinkle with the basil, salt and pepper. Combine the mozzarella cheese, Parmesan cheese and mayonnaise in a bowl and mix well. Spread over the tomatoes. Bake for 30 to 40 minutes or until bubbly. Remove from the oven and let stand for 30 minutes before cutting into wedges to serve.

YIELD: 6 TO 8 SERVINGS

Italian Vegetable Casserole

2 (14-ounce) cans artichoke hearts,
* drained*
Italian bread crumbs
2 (16-ounce) cans whole green beans,
* drained*
Sliced tomatoes
Cavender's seasoning
¹/4 cup grated Parmesan cheese
¹/2 cup shredded Swiss cheese
1 cup mayonnaise
1 cup sour cream
1 small onion, chopped
Butter

Rinse the artichoke hearts; drain. Cut the artichoke hearts into quarters. Sprinkle some of the bread crumbs in a 3-quart baking dish sprayed with nonstick cooking spray. Layer the artichoke heart quarters, green beans and tomato slices in the prepared dish. Sprinkle with Cavender's seasoning, Parmesan cheese and Swiss cheese. Mix the mayonnaise, sour cream and onion in a bowl. Spread over the layers. Sprinkle with the desired amount of bread crumbs. Dot with butter. Bake at 350 degrees for 45 minutes.

YIELD: 8 SERVINGS

1806

The British vessel *Leander* fired on the American ship *Richard*.

Henry Clay became a United States senator from Kentucky

England claimed the right to search American ships on the high seas. The United States objected.

Zebulon M. Pike first saw Pike's Peak on November 15.

James Monroe and William Pinckney were selected to settle the United States dispute with England.

Corn Bread Dressing

4 cups crumbled corn bread
2 cups dry bread crumbs
3¹/2 cups chicken stock
3 eggs, lightly beaten
1 cup milk
1 cup chopped celery
1 cup chopped onion
2 teaspoons salt
¹/2 teaspoon pepper
1 teaspoon sage

Combine the corn bread, bread crumbs and chicken stock in a large bowl and mix well. Stir in the eggs. Add the milk, celery, onion, salt, pepper and sage and mix well. Chill, covered, for 8 to 12 hours to enhance the flavor. Spoon into a well-greased 9×13-inch baking dish. Bake at 375 degrees for 30 to 40 minutes or until set.

YIELD: 10 SERVINGS

Cornmeal Dumplings

1¹/2 cups water
1 cup cornmeal
¹/2 teaspoon salt
1 egg, beaten
Beef or chicken broth

Bring the water to a boil in a saucepan. Add the cornmeal gradually. Cook until thickened, stirring constantly. Stir in the salt. Remove from the heat to cool. Add the egg and mix well. Drop by rounded tablespoonfuls onto a floured surface. Roll into balls. Bring the broth to a boil in a saucepan. Add the cornmeal balls. Cook, covered, for 15 minutes.

YIELD: 4 TO 6 SERVINGS

Note: You may cook these dumplings in turnip greens.

1806

Noah Webster published his compendious dictionary of the English language.

The first stories of George Washington and the cherry tree began to appear.

President Jefferson's grandson, James Madison Randolph, was the first child to be born in the White House.

Russian ships arrived in San Francisco to collect food for starving Russians.

Grits Casserole

3 cups cooked grits
3 eggs, beaten
2 teaspoons grated onion
3 garlic cloves, minced

3 tablespoons heavy cream
1/4 cup (1/2 stick) butter, melted
2 cups grated sharp cheese
Crushed cornflakes

Combine the grits, eggs, onion, garlic, cream and butter in a bowl and mix well. Stir in the cheese. Spoon into a greased baking dish. Sprinkle with crushed cornflakes. Bake at 350 degrees for 45 to 50 minutes or until set.

YIELD: 6 TO 8 SERVINGS

Creamy White Grits

1 cup heavy cream
2 cups milk
1/4 cup quick-cooking grits
2 tablespoons butter

Salt and freshly ground white pepper to
 taste
1 cup freshly grated imported Parmesan
 cheese

Bring the cream and milk to a simmer in a heavy saucepan. Stir in the grits and return to a boil. Reduce the heat. Cook, covered, for 7 minutes, stirring occasionally and adding a small amount of water if the grits begin to separate and turn lumpy. Remove from the heat. Add the butter, salt and white pepper. Stir in the Parmesan cheese.

YIELD: 4 TO 6 SERVINGS

Note: You may make ahead and reheat over low heat or in the microwave.

Slow-Cooker Macaroni and Cheese

1 (8-ounce) package macaroni
1/2 cup (1 stick) butter or margarine, melted
3 cups shredded sharp Cheddar cheese
2 eggs, beaten
1 (12-ounce) can evaporated milk
2 cups milk
Salt and pepper to taste
Shredded sharp Cheddar cheese

Cook the macaroni in a saucepan using the package directions; drain. Pour into a slow cooker. Add the melted butter. Add 3 cups cheese and mix well. Mix the eggs, evaporated milk and milk in a bowl. Pour over the macaroni mixture. Season with salt and pepper and mix well. Sprinkle with cheese. Cook on Low for 3 hours.

YIELD: 4 SERVINGS

1807

British ships were ordered out of all American waters.

The British warship *Leopard* fired on the United States frigate *Chesapeake*.

The British announced that they would pursue their policy of impressing (forcing civilians into military service) Americans even more vigorously.

The first successful flint glass factory was established in Philadelphia.

The first glue factory was established in Boston.

The first soft drink (soda pop) was prepared in Philadelphia.

Cheesy Green Chile Rice

1 cup uncooked rice
2 cups chicken broth
2 tablespoons butter
8 ounces Monterey Jack cheese,
  cut into cubes

1 (4-ounce) can chopped green chiles
1/2 cup milk
2 cups sour cream

Combine the uncooked rice, chicken broth and butter in a bowl and mix well. Spoon into a baking dish. Bake, covered, at 350 degrees for 40 minutes. Combine the cheese, green chiles, milk and sour cream in a bowl and mix well. Fold into the cooked rice. Bake, uncovered, for 30 minutes.

YIELD: 4 TO 6 SERVINGS

Mother's Glazed Apples

This festive dish is beautiful to serve for Christmas dinner.

12 Rome, York or Winesap apples
Lemon juice
Water
4 cups sugar
6 cups water

Juice of 1 lemon
Red food coloring
Cinnamon hearts candy
1/4 cup (1/2 stick) butter

Peel the apples and core. Place immediately into a mixture of lemon juice and water in a bowl to prevent discoloration. Combine the sugar, 6 cups water and juice of 1 lemon in a large skillet and mix well. Bring to a boil. Boil for 45 minutes or until thickened, stirring frequently. Add the food coloring, cinnamon candies and butter and mix well. Arrange the apples in the syrup, spooning the syrup over the apples. Do not crowd. Cook for 30 minutes or until tender. Arrange in a shallow baking dish. Pour the syrup over the apples. Chill, covered, for 8 to 12 hours. Baste with all of the syrup. Bake at 350 degrees for 30 to 40 minutes or until heated through, basting frequently. Remove the apples from the syrup and arrange on a serving platter. Serve hot or at room temperature.

YIELD: 12 SERVINGS

Hot Spiced Fruit

1 (16-ounce) can whole cranberry sauce
1/3 cup sugar
1 tablespoon lemon juice
1/4 teaspoon cinnamon

1/4 teaspoon ground ginger
6 medium pears, peeled, cored, cut into
    wedges
2 oranges, peeled, cut into wedges

Combine the cranberry sauce, sugar, lemon juice, cinnamon and ginger in a saucepan and mix well. Bring to a boil, stirring constantly. Arrange the pears and oranges in a 9×13-inch baking dish. Pour the hot mixture over the top. Bake, covered, at 350 degrees for 40 minutes or until the pears are tender.

YIELD: 6 SERVINGS

Cranberry Orange Apple Relish

2 oranges, rinsed
1 pound fresh cranberries,
    rinsed

2 Cortland or McIntosh apples, rinsed,
    cored
Sugar to taste

Peel 1 orange. Section and remove the seeds. Cut the remaining unpeeled orange into sections and remove the seeds. Force the oranges, cranberries and apples through a food mill into a bowl. Add sugar 1/2 cup at a time, until sweetened to taste. Chill, covered, in the refrigerator until ready to serve.

YIELD: 6 SERVINGS

Note: You may store in the refrigerator for up to 2 weeks.

Sweet Chowchow

This recipe is over one hundred years old.

1 water bucket green tomatoes
1 (4¹/2-pound) head cabbage
4 large onions
4 large bell peppers
4 cups vinegar
5 cups sugar, or to taste
4¹/2 teaspoons salt
3 or 4 teaspoons pepper
1 (.9-ounce) jar allspice

Rinse the green tomatoes, cabbage, onions and bell peppers and cut into quarters. Force through a food grinder until ground. Place in a large stockpot. Add the vinegar, sugar, salt and pepper. Tie the allspice in a cheesecloth bag. Add to the vegetable mixture. Bring to a heavy boil and reduce the heat. Simmer for 2¹/2 hours, stirring frequently. Discard the cheesecloth bag. Ladle into hot sterilized 1-pint jars, leaving ¹/2 inch headspace; secure with 2-piece lids. Process in a boiling water bath for 10 minutes.

YIELD: 16 TO 18 PINTS

Note: You may add some chopped hot pepper.

1808

Napoleon ordered all United States ships in French ports seized.

James Monroe returned to the United States from his European mission.

The Osage Treaty was signed. The Osage Indians ceded nearly all of what is now Missouri and Arkansas north of the Missouri River and moved to the reservation along the Arkansas River in what is now Oklahoma.

John J. Astor established the American Fur Company, with head-quarters on Mackinac Island, and soon established a monopoly on Canadian fur.

The American Academy of Fine Arts was founded in New York.

Pigtails for men went out of fashion at about this time.

Cheesy Corn Spoon Bread

1 medium onion, chopped
1/4 cup (1/2 stick) butter or margarine
2 eggs
2 cups sour cream
1 (15-ounce) can whole kernel corn,
   drained
1 (14-ounce) can cream-style corn

1/4 teaspoon salt
1/4 teaspoon pepper
1 (8-ounce) package corn bread muffin
   mix
1 medium jalapeño, minced
2 cups shredded Cheddar cheese

Sauté the onion in the butter in a skillet until tender. Beat the eggs in a bowl. Add the sour cream, whole kernel corn, cream-style corn, salt and pepper to the eggs and mix well. Stir in the corn bread mix just until combined. Fold in the sautéed onion, chile and 1 1/2 cups of the cheese. Spoon into a greased shallow 3-quart baking dish. Sprinkle with the remaining 1/2 cup cheese. Bake at 375 degrees for 35 to 40 minutes or until a wooden pick inserted near the center comes out clean. Cool slightly before serving.

YIELD: 12 TO 15 SERVINGS

Spoon Bread

1 1/2 cups water
2 cups milk
1 1/2 cups cornmeal
1 1/4 teaspoons salt

1 1/2 teaspoons sugar
2 tablespoons butter
5 eggs
1 tablespoon baking powder

Bring the water and milk to a simmer in a saucepan. Add the cornmeal, salt, sugar and butter. Cook over medium heat for 5 minutes or until thickened, stirring constantly. Remove from the heat. Beat the eggs and baking powder in a mixing bowl until light and fluffy. Add to the cornmeal mixture and mix well. Pour into a greased large shallow baking dish. Bake at 350 degrees for 45 to 50 minutes or until set. Serve hot.

YIELD: 8 SERVINGS

Heritage Side Dishes

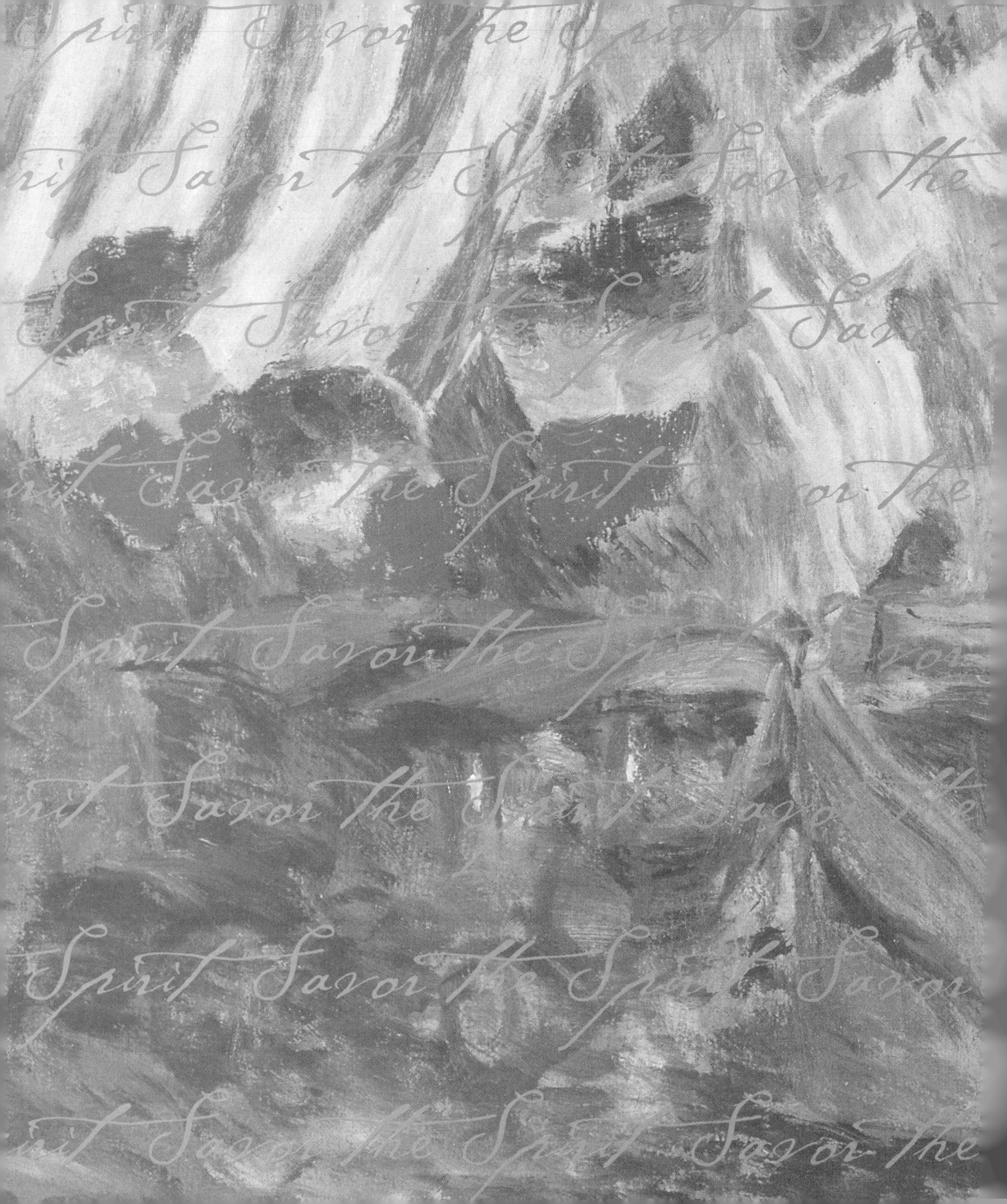
Savor the Spirit

Just Desserts

THE WAR YEARS

1809–1815

1809

James Madison was inaugurated as the fourth president. George Clinton was his vice president.

Thomas Jefferson retired to Monticello, his home in Virginia, after forty-four years of continuous public service.

James Monroe was named secretary of state.

John Quincy Adams was named minister to Russia.

Abraham Lincoln was born in Hodgenville, Kentucky.

The first railroad for freight transport was established in Pennsylvania.

Ephraim McDowell performed the first abdominal surgical operation in Kentucky.

At this time there were thirty daily newspapers in the United States.

Sour Cream Cheesecake

1 (16-ounce) package graham crackers,
   crumbled
1/2 cup sugar
1/2 cup (1 stick) butter, melted
24 ounces cream cheese, softened
4 eggs
1 cup sugar
1 tablespoon vanilla extract
2 cups sour cream
1/2 cup sugar
1/2 teaspoon vanilla extract

Combine the graham cracker crumbs, 1/2 cup sugar and the butter in a bowl and mix well. Press over the bottom and 3/4 of the way up the side of a 91/2- or 10-inch springform pan.

Process the cream cheese, eggs, 1 cup sugar and 1 tablespoon vanilla in a food processor until smooth. Pour into the prepared pan. Bake at 350 degrees for 50 minutes. Cool in the pan for 15 minutes. Combine the sour cream, 1/2 cup sugar and 1/2 teaspoon vanilla in a bowl and mix well. Spread over the top of the cheesecake. Bake for 10 minutes. Remove from the oven to cool. Chill until ready to serve.

YIELD: 15 SERVINGS

Pumpkin Cheesecake

1 1/2 cups ground gingersnap cookies
1 1/2 cups pecan halves, toasted
1/4 cup packed brown sugar
1/4 cup (1/2 stick) unsalted butter, melted
32 ounces cream cheese, softened
4 eggs
1 2/3 cups sugar

1 1/2 cups canned solid-pack pumpkin
1/4 cup heavy cream
1 teaspoon cinnamon
1 teaspoon allspice
3/4 cup whipping cream
3 tablespoons confectioners' sugar
Cinnamon to taste

Process the ground cookies, pecans and brown sugar in a food processor until finely ground. Add the butter and process until combined. Press over the bottom and 2 3/4 inches up the side of a 9-inch springform pan.

Beat the cream cheese, eggs and sugar in a large mixing bowl until light. Chill, tightly covered, in the refrigerator. Add the pumpkin, 1/4 cup heavy cream, 1 teaspoon cinnamon and allspice and beat well. Pour into the prepared pan. Bake at 350 degrees for 1 1/4 hours or until the top browns and the center moves slightly in the center when shaken. Remove to a wire rack. Let cool for 10 minutes. Run a sharp knife around the edge to loosen the cheesecake from the side of the pan. Chill, tightly covered, for 8 to 12 hours.

Beat 3/4 cup whipping cream, confectioners' sugar and cinnamon to taste in a mixing bowl until soft peaks form. To serve, release the side of the springform pan and remove. Pipe the whipped cream mixture decoratively over the top of the cheesecake.

YIELD: 15 SERVINGS

Flag of the War of 1812

The flag of the War of 1812 is the flag of the United States of America with fifteen stars and fifteen stripes. Admission of Vermont and Kentucky added two states to the union, for which two stars and two stripes were added to the original flag.

Crème Brûlée

2 cups heavy cream
4 egg yolks
1/4 cup confectioners' sugar

1 teaspoon vanilla extract
2 tablespoons confectioners' sugar

Heat the cream in a double boiler over hot water to just below the boiling point. Combine the egg yolks, 1/4 cup confectioners' sugar and the vanilla in a mixing bowl and beat well. Add the warm cream and mix well. Pour into a shallow baking dish. Place the dish in a larger dish. Add enough hot water to the larger dish to come halfway up the side of the smaller dish. Bake at 300 degrees for 1 hour or until set. Let stand until cool. Chill, covered, for 3 to 12 hours. Sprinkle the top with 2 tablespoons confectioners' sugar. Broil until the confectioners' sugar is caramelized. Chill until ready to serve.

YIELD: 4 TO 6 SERVINGS

James Madison

James Madison, a native Virginian, served his state in many capacities. He advocated a strong central government and secured the passage of Thomas Jefferson's landmark religious freedom bill. He was instrumental in adding the Bill of Rights for which history has dubbed him "Father of the Constitution." Madison was elected president in 1809 having previously served as Jefferson's secretary of state. When Madison was president, the War of 1812 broke out. The problems between America and England had never been solved. Though England repealed the Order in Council concerning shipping, it was too late for the war to be avoided. The plan was already in motion for the Battle of New Orleans. This occurred because there were no forms of immediate communication as we have today. His wife, Dolley, was known for years throughout Washington as the official hostess. Both he and Dolley had to flee Washington when the British burned it in 1814. He was Jefferson's successor as rector of the University of Virginia 1826–1836.

Orange Trifle

8 navel oranges
1/4 cup Cointreau
1 tablespoon grated orange zest
1/2 cup sugar
1/2 teaspoon salt
3 tablespoons cornstarch
2 1/2 cups milk
4 egg yolks, beaten
1 teaspoon vanilla extract

1 tablespoon grated orange zest
2 cups whipping cream, whipped
2/3 cup (4 ounces) chocolate chips
1 1/2 cups Pepperidge Farm Old-Fashioned
   Lemon Nut Crunch Cookies
1 (16-ounce) all butter pound cake
3/4 cup sweet orange marmalade
Sprigs of fresh mint

Peel the oranges. Cut 7 of the oranges into sections and place in a medium bowl, discarding the white pith. Squeeze the juice from the remaining orange over the orange sections. Add the orange liqueur and 1 tablespoon orange zest. Let stand for 30 minutes. Reserve 12 of the orange sections for garnish. Drain the remaining orange sections, reserving the liquid.

Combine the sugar, salt and cornstarch in a 2-quart microwave-safe dish. Whisk in the milk and 1/2 cup of the reserved orange liquid. Microwave on High at 2-minute intervals for 6 minutes or until slightly thickened. Add the egg yolks and whisk to blend. Microwave on Medium-High for 1 minute and whisk. Let stand until cool. Stir in the vanilla and 1 tablespoon orange zest. Pour into a medium bowl. Fold in the whipped cream.

Microwave the chocolate chips in a microwave-safe dish on Medium for 2 minutes or until melted. Arrange the cookies on a cookie sheet. Drizzle with the melted chocolate. Let stand until the chocolate hardens. Crumble the cookies.

Cut the pound cake into slices. Layer the pound cake, orange marmalade, remaining reserved orange liquid, orange sections, crumbled cookies and the orange cream 1/2 at a time in a trifle bowl. Garnish with the reserved orange sections and sprigs of fresh mint.

YIELD: 20 TO 25 SERVINGS

Commodore Johnston Blakely
Johnston Blakely quickly rose through the ranks of the United States Navy and was given command of the USS *Enterprise* in 1811 followed by the new sloop USS *Wasp*. He captured five British merchant vessels and a total of fourteen ships in five months. He sent one ship, HMS *Atlanta*, back to Savannah, Georgia, with a prize crew for which he won accolades. Later, he and his ship were lost at sea.

1810

The third United States census recorded a total population of 7,239,881 in the seventeen states.

Napoleon continued seizing United States ships in French ports.

Inhabitants of western Florida revolted and captured the fort at Baton Rouge, Louisiana.

The first carpet factory was started in Frederick City, Maryland.

The first silk mill was established in Mansfield, Connecticut.

The mailbox was invented by Thomas Brown.

The first regular orchestra in the United States was organized in Boston.

Chocolate Snowball

8 ounces semisweet chocolate
2 teaspoons instant coffee granules
1 cup sugar
1/2 cup boiling water
1 cup (2 sticks) unsalted butter, softened,
  cut into pieces
4 eggs
1 tablespoon brandy or amaretto
1/8 teaspoon salt
1 cup whipping cream
2 tablespoons sugar
1 tablespoon brandy or amaretto
Shaved chocolate

Line a 5-cup round glass baking dish with a double thickness of foil, leaving the foil slightly taller than the dish. Grease the foil. Process the chocolate, coffee granules and 1 cup sugar in a food processor until the chocolate is finely chopped. Add the boiling water gradually, processing constantly until smooth. Add the butter and blend well. Add the eggs, 1 tablespoon brandy and salt and process well. Pour into the prepared dish. Bake at 450 degrees for 45 minutes or until a thick crust forms on the top. Let stand to cool. Chill thoroughly.

Invert onto a cake stand or platter. Remove the foil. Beat the whipping cream, 2 tablespoons sugar and 1 tablespoon brandy in a mixing bowl until soft peaks form. Spread over the top and side of the baked layer. Sprinkle with shaved chocolate. Cut into wedges to serve. Garnish each serving with sprigs of fresh mint, strawberries, raspberries or candied violets.

YIELD: 8 TO 10 SERVINGS

Ice Box Cake

2 cups (12 ounces) chocolate chips
3 tablespoons water
1/2 cup sugar
3 egg yolks, lightly beaten
3 egg whites, stiffly beaten

1 angel food cake, cut into
 thin slices
Whipped cream
Grated chocolate

Melt the chocolate chips in the water in a double boiler over hot water. Add the sugar and egg yolks. Cook for 5 minutes or until thickened, stirring constantly. Remove from the heat. Fold in the stiffly beaten egg whites. Line the bottom of a buttered dish with cake slices. Layer the chocolate mixture and remaining cake slices 1/2 at a time in the prepared dish. Cover the top cake layer with whipped cream. Chill, covered, for 8 to 12 hours. Sprinkle with grated chocolate just before serving.

YIELD: 15 SERVINGS

Rainbow Frozen Cake

1 angel food cake, cut into cubes
1 (3-ounce) package strawberry gelatin
1 (3-ounce) package lime gelatin
1 (3-ounce) package orange gelatin
1 (10-ounce) package frozen strawberries,
 partially thawed

1/2 to 1 gallon ice cream, softened
1 (10-ounce) package frozen blueberries
1 (11-ounce) can mandarin oranges,
 drained

Divide the cake cubes into 3 equal portions. Place each portion in separate bowls, pinching each cake piece. Sprinkle a different flavor of gelatin into each bowl and toss to mix well. Layer the strawberry cake pieces, strawberries, 1/3 of the ice cream, lime cake pieces, blueberries, 1/2 of the remaining ice cream, orange cake pieces, mandarin oranges and remaining ice cream in a tube pan. Freeze until firm. To serve, loosen the cake from the pan by wrapping in a hot cloth. Invert onto a cake plate.

YIELD: 15 SERVINGS

Berry Cobbler

3 cups berries
1 cup sugar
1/4 teaspoon almond extract
1 1/3 cups flour
2 1/2 teaspoons baking powder
1 tablespoon sugar

1 teaspoon salt
1/3 cup shortening
1 egg, beaten
1/2 cup milk
2 tablespoons sugar

Combine the berries, 1 cup sugar and almond extract in a bowl and toss to mix. Spoon into a baking dish and place in a 400-degree oven. Sift the flour, baking powder, 1 tablespoon sugar and salt into a bowl. Cut in the shortening until crumbly. Add the egg and milk and mix well. Spread over the preheated berries. Sprinkle with 2 tablespoons sugar. Bake at 400 degrees for 30 to 40 minutes or until the top is golden brown.

YIELD: 8 SERVINGS

Blueberry Crisp

3/4 cup flour
3/4 cup packed brown sugar
6 tablespoons butter

4 cups blueberries
1/4 cup port

Mix the flour and brown sugar in a bowl. Cut in the butter until crumbly. Arrange the blueberries in a 1-quart baking dish. Pour the wine over the blueberries. Spread the flour mixture over the top. Bake at 375 degrees for 30 to 40 minutes or until the top is golden brown. Serve over ice cream.

YIELD: 8 TO 10 SERVINGS

Major General William Carroll

Andrew Jackson referred to William Carroll as "the best Brigade Major in the armies of the United States—he ought and he must be at the head of a regiment." Carroll displayed initiative, leadership and courage during the Creek War and was made major general of the Tennessee militia Second Division. He played a pivotal role in the victories of the southern campaigns, especially New Orleans.

Cranberry Apple Crisp

Immortalized in Longfellow's famous book, the Wayside Inn in Sudbury, Massachusetts, is America's oldest operating inn. Established in 1716, the tavern was later the meeting place of the Sudbury Minutemen as they gathered to march to Lexington and Concord on April 19, 1775. Often served warm with ice cream, this dessert is still enjoyed today by modern travelers.

2 cups whole cranberry sauce	2 teaspoons cinnamon
1/2 cup sugar	1 cup (2 sticks) butter
2 cups flour	1 tablespoon honey
1 cup sugar	8 apples, peeled, cored, sliced

Combine the cranberry sauce and 1/2 cup sugar in a saucepan and mix well. Bring to a boil over medium heat, stirring frequently. Remove from the heat to cool. Mix the flour, 1 cup sugar and cinnamon in a bowl. Cut in the butter until crumbly. Add the honey and mix well.

Spread the cranberry mixture in a baking dish. Layer the apples over the cranberry mixture. Spread the topping over the apples. Bake at 350 degrees for 30 to 45 minutes or until brown.

YIELD: 10 TO 12 SERVINGS

Captain Thomas MacDonough, Jr.

During the years leading up to the War of 1812, the British began impressing American sailors. While in Liverpool, England, MacDonough was impressed into the British navy. He was taken on board a British ship and assigned sleeping quarters with the corporal of the guard. He made his escape by switching uniforms and Thomas swore, "If I live, I'll make England remember the day she impressed an American soldier"... and he did! During the War of 1812, Americans under his command were able to thwart the British invasion of the northern United States in a decisive naval battle on Lake Champlain.

1811

The United States frigate *President* defeated the British ship *Little Belt*.

The United States seized western Florida over British protests.

A bounty of sixteen dollars was offered to army recruits, along with three months' extra pay and 160 acres of land, upon discharge.

This was the first year that United States exports exceeded imports.

The worst earthquake in American history rocked the Ohio and Mississippi valleys.

Regular steamboat service began on the Mississippi River between New Orleans and Natchez.

Apple Dumplings

This recipe was handed down from Mary Anna Weigandt Page, wife of William Tyler Page, the author of The American's Creed.

2 cups flour
4 teaspoons baking powder
1 teaspoon salt
1/4 cup shortening
1 cup milk
6 apples, peeled, cored
Sugar and cinnamon to taste

Sift the flour, baking powder and salt into a bowl. Cut in the shortening until crumbly. Add the milk gradually, stirring to form a smooth dough. Divide the dough into 6 equal portions. Roll each portion into a circle large enough to cover 1 apple.

Place an apple in the center of each circle. Fill the centers of the apples with sugar and cinnamon. Dampen the edge of each circle with water and fold over the apple, sealing to enclose. Arrange on a greased baking sheet. Bake at 350 degrees for 30 minutes or until the apples are tender. Serve with hard sauce or liquid sauce.

YIELD: 6 SERVINGS

Fruit Kuchen

1¹/4 cups flour
1 teaspoon sugar
1 teaspoon baking powder
¹/2 teaspoon salt
¹/2 cup (1 stick) butter
1 egg yolk
2 tablespoons milk
Berries
Sugar
Sliced peaches
Sliced apples

Ground cloves or nutmeg (optional)
³/4 cup sugar
1¹/2 tablespoons flour
¹/4 teaspoon cinnamon
2 tablespoons butter
3 cups sliced rhubarb
³/4 cup sugar
2 tablespoons flour
2 tablespoons butter
2 egg yolks, or 1 egg

Mix 1¹/4 cups flour, 1 teaspoon sugar, baking powder and salt in a bowl. Cut in ¹/2 cup butter until crumbly. Beat 1 egg yolk and the milk in a small bowl. Add to the dry ingredients and mix well. Spread over the bottom and up the side of a buttered baking dish. Fill with berries and sprinkle with enough sugar to lightly coat. Layer the peaches and apples over the berries. Cover with sugar. Sprinkle with ground cloves. Mix ³/4 cup sugar, 1¹/2 tablespoons flour and ¹/4 teaspoon cinnamon in a bowl. Cut in 2 tablespoons butter until crumbly. Spread over the fruit.

Scald the rhubarb in boiling water in a saucepan. Remove from the heat and let stand for 5 minutes; drain. Mix ³/4 cup sugar and 2 tablespoons flour in a bowl. Cut in 2 tablespoons butter until crumbly. Add 2 egg yolks and mix well. Stir in the drained rhubarb. Spread over the layers. Bake at 375 degrees for 45 minutes or until set. Remove from the dish. Serve hot or cold with ice cream.

YIELD: 8 TO 10 SERVINGS

General John Stricker
John Stricker played a vital role in the American defense of Baltimore during the War of 1812. He was a brigadier general in charge of the third brigade and responsible for delaying the advance of the British forces into Baltimore. The defenders of Baltimore successfully repelled several attacks on the city. Since they were unable to bomb Fort McHenry into submission, and facing a superior force protected by well-built defenses, the British decided to retreat. After the humiliating sack of the nation's capital, this was an important source of pride for the United States.

Stewed Berries with Ice Cream

3 cups fresh raspberries
2 cups fresh blueberries
1 1/2 cups sugar

3/4 cup water
2 tablespoons framboise
2 pints vanilla ice cream

Combine 2 cups of the raspberries, blueberries, sugar and water in a medium saucepan. Bring to a boil and reduce the heat. Cook over medium to low heat for 10 to 12 minutes or until syrupy and the berries have released their juices, stirring occasionally. Remove from the heat. Stir in the remaining raspberries and framboise. Ladle 3/4 cup stewed berries into each serving bowl. Top with a large scoop of ice cream.

YIELD: 6 SERVINGS

Chocolate Mint Ice Cream

2 eggs
3 cups heavy cream
1 cup milk
1/2 cup sugar
1/4 cup light corn syrup

1 teaspoon vanilla extract
1/4 teaspoon salt
1/3 cup green crème de menthe
Few drops of green food coloring
2 ounces semisweet chocolate, shaved

Beat the eggs in a mixing bowl at high speed for 4 minutes or until light. Add the cream, milk, sugar, corn syrup, vanilla and salt and beat until the sugar is dissolved. Stir in the crème de menthe and food coloring. Pour into a 1-gallon ice cream freezer container. Freeze using the manufacturer's directions. Remove the dasher and fold in the chocolate. Pack and let stand to blend flavors.

YIELD: 8 SERVINGS

General Peter B. Porter

Peter B. Porter was the brigadier general of the New York militia who participated in the crossing of the Niagara River, the capture of Fort Erie, and later in causing a British retreat at The Battle of Chippewa. Porter was awarded a gold medal for his successful attack against the British artillery that was besieging Fort Erie.

Grandmother's Ice Cream

8 cups milk
2 cups sugar
4 eggs
2 tablespoons flour

Pinch of salt
2 tablespoons vanilla extract
1 cup heavy cream

Scald the milk in a saucepan. Mix the sugar, eggs, flour and salt in a bowl. Add to the hot milk. Cook until thickened, stirring constantly. Stir in the vanilla. Remove from the heat to cool. Stir in the cream. Pour into an ice cream freezer container. Freeze using the manufacturer's directions.

YIELD: 8 SERVINGS

Boiled Custard

When the war with the Creek Indians commenced in 1813, a Winston family council was held to determine which of the seven brothers and brothers-in-law should be selected to remain at home to protect the young northern Alabama families. William Winston was chosen on account of his firmness and prudence. He was elected in June of 1815 as one of the three delegates representing Madison County to the Legislature of the Mississippi Territory. This recipe was handed down in the family through his daughter.

10 tablespoons sugar
2 tablespoons flour
Pinch of salt
6 egg yolks

8 cups milk
6 egg whites
10 tablespoons sugar
3/4 teaspoon vanilla extract

Mix 10 tablespoons sugar, flour and salt together. Add gradually to the egg yolks in a saucepan, stirring constantly. Stir in the milk gradually. Bring to a boil. Cook until thickened, stirring constantly. Remove from the heat to cool. Beat the egg whites in a mixing bowl until soft peaks form. Add 10 tablespoons sugar gradually, beating constantly until stiff peaks form. Stir the vanilla into the cooled custard. Fold in the egg whites.

YIELD: 8 SERVINGS

Frigate Constellation

The *Constellation* is a ship of the United States Navy and one of the most famous vessels ever built. She was constructed in Baltimore in 1794 to be powerful enough to protect American Commerce overseas. She was launched in 1797. At the outbreak of the War of 1812, the *Constellation* was placed under the command of Captain William Bainbridge. She was decommissioned in 1955 and returned to her native waters at Baltimore.

Fresh Apple Cake

2 cups flour
1¹/2 teaspoons baking soda
2 teaspoons cinnamon
1 teaspoon salt
4 cups sliced peeled apples
2 cups sugar

2 eggs
³/4 cup vegetable oil
2 teaspoons vanilla extract
1 cup chopped pecans
Sauce for Fresh Apple Cake (below)

Sift the flour, baking soda, cinnamon and salt together. Combine the apples and sugar in a large bowl and toss to mix. Add the flour mixture and mix well. Beat the eggs, oil and vanilla in a small bowl. Add to the apple mixture and stir until thoroughly moistened. Stir in the pecans. Spoon into a greased 9×13-inch cake pan. Bake at 350 degrees for 50 minutes or until the cake springs back when lightly touched. Serve with warm Sauce for Fresh Apple Cake.

YIELD: 12 TO 15 SERVINGS

Sauce for Fresh Apple Cake

1 cup sugar
¹/2 cup (1 stick) butter or margarine

¹/2 cup heavy cream or evaporated milk
1 teaspoon vanilla extract

Combine the sugar, butter, cream and vanilla in a saucepan. Bring to a boil over medium-high heat, stirring constantly. Remove from the heat. Cool for 3 minutes and serve.

YIELD: 12 TO 15 SERVINGS

Commodore John Rodgers
As commander of the northern squadron of the United States coast, John Rodgers immediately went to sea upon the outbreak of the War of 1812, and participated in four wartime cruises. The cruises from the Caribbean to Norway netted nearly two dozen captures of enemy ships and $175,000 in gold and silver.

Carrot Cake

2 cups flour
2 teaspoons baking soda
2 teaspoons cinnamon
1 teaspoon salt
2 cups sugar
4 eggs
2 (8-ounce) jars junior baby food carrots
1 (8-ounce) can crushed pineapple, drained
1 cup raisins
1 cup vegetable oil
1 teaspoon vanilla extract
1 cup chopped pecans or walnuts
Cream Cheese Frosting (below)

Sift the flour, baking soda, cinnamon and salt together. Beat the sugar and eggs in a large mixing bowl until smooth. Add the carrots, pineapple, raisins, oil and vanilla and mix well. Add the flour mixture and mix well. Fold in the pecans. Pour into a greased 9×13-inch cake pan. Bake at 350 degrees in the upper half of the oven for 45 minutes or until the cake tests done. Cool on a wire rack. Spread Cream Cheese Frosting over the top of the cooled cake. Store, covered, in the refrigerator.

YIELD: 15 SERVINGS

Cream Cheese Frosting

1/2 cup (1 stick) butter, softened
4 ounces cream cheese, softened
1/2 teaspoon vanilla extract
1/2 (16-ounce) package confectioners' sugar

Cream the butter, cream cheese and vanilla in a mixing bowl until light and fluffy. Add the confectioners' sugar and beat until smooth.

YIELD: 15 SERVINGS

1812

The United States declared war against Great Britain.

Louisiana became the eighteenth state.

Congress authorized the first issuance of United States War Bonds.

The United States ship *Old Ironsides* defeated the British ships *Guerriere* and *Java*.

President Madison refused the services of Andrew Jackson, so Jackson organized an independent military corps.

Congress placed an embargo on American shipping.

The Seminole War was fought in Florida.

Detroit surrendered to the British.

President Madison was authorized to call up 100,000 men for six-month service terms.

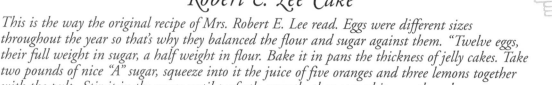

Robert E. Lee Cake

This is the way the original recipe of Mrs. Robert E. Lee read. Eggs were different sizes throughout the year so that's why they balanced the flour and sugar against them. "Twelve eggs, their full weight in sugar, a half weight in flour. Bake it in pans the thickness of jelly cakes. Take two pounds of nice "A" sugar, squeeze into it the juice of five oranges and three lemons together with the pulp. Stir it in the sugar until perfectly smooth, then spread it over the cakes as you would do jelly—-putting one above another till the whole of the sugar is used up."

6 egg whites
1 cup sugar
6 egg yolks
1½ teaspoons grated lemon zest
1 tablespoon lemon juice

1 cup sifted self-rising flour
1 (4-ounce) package lemon pudding and
  pie filling mix
1 (16-ounce) can ready-to-use white
  frosting

Beat the egg whites in a mixing bowl until foamy. Add the sugar 2 tablespoons at a time, beating until stiff peaks form. Beat the egg yolks in a mixing bowl until thick and pale yellow. Add the lemon zest and lemon juice. Fold in the beaten egg whites. Sift the flour ½ cup at a time over the batter, folding in gently after each addition. Spoon into three greased and waxed paper-lined 8-inch round cake pans. Bake at 350 degrees for 35 to 45 minutes or until the layers spring back when lightly touched. Invert the pans and cool completely before removing the layers from the pans.

Prepare the pudding and pie filling mix using the package directions. Spread between the cake layers. Spread the white frosting over the top and side of the cake.

YIELD: 12 SERVINGS

Captain Stephen Decatur, Jr.
Considered the foremost naval hero of his time, Stephen Decatur was, at the age of 25, the youngest captain in United States naval history. He was in command of the *United States* in 1812 when they captured the British frigate, *Macedonian*, in a ferocious sea battle. He sailed back into the port of New London with his prize and received great acclaim for his prowess at sea.

Mississippi Mud Cake

1 cup (2 sticks) butter or margarine
1/2 cup baking cocoa
2 cups sugar
4 eggs, lightly beaten
1 1/2 cups flour

1/4 teaspoon salt
1 teaspoon vanilla extract
1 cup chopped pecans (optional)
4 cups miniature marshmallows
Chocolate Frosting (below)

Melt the butter with the baking cocoa in a medium saucepan over medium heat, stirring frequently. Pour into a large mixing bowl. Add the sugar and eggs. Beat at medium speed until blended. Add the flour, salt and vanilla and beat well. Stir in the pecans. Spoon into a lightly greased 9×13-inch cake pan. Bake at 350 degrees for 35 minutes. Remove from the oven and sprinkle with the marshmallows. Spread Chocolate Frosting immediately over the marshmallows. Cool in the pan on a wire rack. Chill in the refrigerator. Cut into squares to serve.

YIELD: 15 SERVINGS

Chocolate Frosting

1/2 cup (1 stick) butter or margarine,
    melted
1/3 cup baking cocoa
1/4 teaspoon salt

1/2 cup milk
1/2 teaspoon vanilla extract
1 (16-ounce) package confectioners' sugar,
    sifted

Combine the butter, baking cocoa, salt, milk and vanilla in a large mixing bowl and mix well. Add the confectioners' sugar and beat until smooth, adding an additional tablespoon of milk if needed for a spreadable consistency.

YIELD: 2 CUPS

Just Desserts

1813

President Madison was inaugurated for his second term. Elbridge Gerry was his vice president.

The British ship *Peacock* was captured by the United States ship *Hornet*, and the British *Boxer* was taken by the United States *Enterprise*.

The Peoria Indian War was fought in Illinois.

Captain Lawrence of the *Chesapeake* cried the famous words, "Don't give up the ship."

The Creek Indian War of 1813–1814 was fought in Alabama.

Special White Fruitcake

1 cup flaked coconut
1 (15-ounce) package golden raisins
1 pound pecans, finely chopped
1 cup chopped red candied cherries
1 1/2 cups chopped green candied cherries
1/2 cup flour
2 cups (4 sticks) butter, softened
2 cups sugar
6 egg yolks
3 1/2 cups flour
1 (2-ounce) bottle rum extract
6 egg whites, stiffly beaten
Honey
1 jigger bourbon
1 jigger rum
1 jigger brandy
Red and green candied cherries

Mix the coconut, raisins, pecans, chopped red candied cherries, chopped green candied cherries and 1/2 cup flour in a bowl. Cream the butter and sugar in a mixing bowl until light and fluffy. Add the egg yolks one at a time, beating well after each addition. Stir in the fruit mixture. Stir in 3 1/2 cups flour and rum extract. Fold in the stiffly beaten egg whites. Spoon into a well-greased 10-inch tube pan.

Bake at 300 degrees for 2 to 2 1/2 hours. Brush with honey. Bake for 30 minutes longer or until the cake tests done. Remove the cake from the pan and wrap in cheesecloth. Place in an airtight container. Pour the bourbon, rum and brandy over the cake. Cover and let ripen for 3 to 4 weeks. Garnish with red and green candied cherries before serving.

YIELD: 16 SERVINGS

Dolley Madison's Soft Gingerbread

Dolley Madison referred to this recipe as "the Jefferson gingerbread" and was very fond of it. She gave the recipe to Martha Washington, who meticulously recorded it for posterity. The recipe was preserved in the White House files and many other First Ladies have used it.

2¼ cups flour
4 teaspoons ground ginger
1 tablespoon cinnamon
1¼ teaspoons baking soda
¼ cup hot water
1 cup molasses
⅔ cup beef drippings or lard
¾ cup hot water
Confectioners' sugar

Sift the flour, ginger and cinnamon together. Dissolve the baking soda in ¼ cup hot water in a small bowl. Combine the molasses and beef drippings in a large bowl and mix well. Add the baking soda mixture and mix well. Add ¾ cup hot water and the flour mixture alternately, beating well after each addition. Pour into a shallow well-greased cake pan. Bake at 350 degrees for 25 to 30 minutes or until a wooden pick inserted in the center comes out clean. Sprinkle with confectioners' sugar.

YIELD: 15 SERVINGS

James Madison

1813

Buffalo, New York, was completely destroyed by British and Indian soldiers.

At the Battle of Lake Erie, O. H. Perry spoke the famous words, "We have met the enemy and they are ours."

Russia offered to mediate between the United States and Great Britain to end the war.

Congress limited the United States Army to 58,000 men.

Just Desserts

Sour Cream Chocolate Chip Cake

1¹/3 cups flour
1¹/2 teaspoons baking powder
1 teaspoon baking soda
1 teaspoon cinnamon
6 tablespoons butter or margarine,
    softened

1 cup sugar
2 eggs
1 cup sour cream
1 cup (6 ounces) semisweet
    chocolate chips
1 tablespoon sugar

Mix the flour, baking powder, baking soda and cinnamon together. Cream the butter and 1 cup sugar in a mixing bowl until light and fluffy. Add the eggs one at a time, beating well after each addition. Add the flour mixture and beat well. Beat in the sour cream. Pour into a greased and floured 9×13-inch cake pan. Sprinkle the chocolate chips over the top. Sprinkle with 1 tablespoon sugar. Bake at 350 degrees for 35 minutes or until the cake begins to pull from the sides of the pan. Serve warm or at room temperature.

YIELD: 10 TO 12 SERVINGS

USS Constitution

Kentucky Stack Cake

4 cups flour
2 teaspoons baking powder
1 teaspoon baking soda
1/2 teaspoon salt
1/2 teaspoon each of 2 or 3 kinds of
    favorite spices, such as cinnamon,
    cloves, allspice or nutmeg
3/4 cup shortening or butter

1 cup sugar
1 cup molasses
3 eggs
1 cup buttermilk
1 teaspoon lemon extract
1 teaspoon vanilla extract
3 cups thick applesauce
Favorite Frosting

Sift the flour, baking powder, baking soda, salt and spices together. Cream the shortening and sugar in a mixing bowl until light and fluffy. Add the molasses and beat well. Add the eggs one at a time, beating well after each addition. Add the buttermilk and flavorings alternately with the flour mixture, beating well after each addition. The batter will be stiff. Divide the batter into six equal portions. Pat each portion into a nonstick 8-inch round cake pan. Bake at 350 degrees for 18 minutes. Cool in the pans for 10 minutes. Remove to wire racks to cool completely. Spread the applesauce between the layers. Frost with your favorite frosting.

YIELD: 16 SERVINGS

USS Constitution

The USS *Constitution* was completed in 1797 and gained the nickname *Old Ironsides* during the War of 1812. The commander of the frigate, Isaac Hull, led her into many sea battles. One in particular was against the English warship *Guerriere*. A sailor was allegedly shot as a result of British guns bouncing off the *Constitution's* sturdy sides. The sailor exclaimed that the ship had sides of iron. This assessment of the ship's toughness was reflected in a poem by Oliver Wendell Holmes, "Old Ironsides." She was one of the most famous vessels in the United States Navy.

After the announcement that the USS *Constitution* was unseaworthy and would be destroyed, the public demanded that she be rebuilt. In 1833, restoration was complete and she was put out to sea. In 1855, she was put out of commission and used as a training ship. By 1877, she was restored once again. Finally, in 1897, she was dry-docked and made a memorial. In the 1930s, she was once again reconditioned and toured the United States ports. She came back for the last time to the Boston Naval Shipyard in 1934 where she is today.

Orange Slice Cake

3 cups flour
1 teaspoon baking soda
1/2 (16-ounce) package orange slice candy
1 (8-ounce) package pitted dates
1 cup chopped pecans
1/2 cup flour
2 cups sugar

1 cup (2 sticks) butter or margarine,
   softened
4 eggs
1/2 cup buttermilk
1 cup flaked coconut
2/3 cup orange juice
2 cups confectioners' sugar

Mix 3 cups flour and the baking soda together. Cut the candy and dates into small pieces. Combine the candy, dates, pecans and 1/2 cup flour in a bowl and toss to coat. Cream the sugar and butter in a mixing bowl until light and fluffy. Add the eggs one at a time, beating well after each addition. Add the flour mixture, buttermilk, coconut and candy mixture alternately, beating well after each addition. Spoon into a greased tube pan. Bake at 250 degrees for 2 hours. Mix the orange juice and confectioners' sugar in a bowl until smooth. Spoon over the hot cake. Let stand for 8 to 12 hours before slicing to enhance the flavors.

YIELD: 10 TO 12 SERVINGS

Commodore Isaac Hull
His first major encounter during the War of 1812 was as commander of the *Constitution*, which was pursued for three days by a British squadron. By exhibiting imaginative seamanship, he was able to elude capture. He won a gold medal for winning a hard fought sea engagement with the HMS *Guerriere*. Five ships in the United States Navy have been named for Commodore Hull.

Oatmeal Cake

1 1/4 cups boiling water
1 cup quick-cooking oats
1/2 cup (1 stick) butter, softened
1 cup packed brown sugar
1 cup sugar
2 eggs
1 1/2 cups flour
1 teaspoon baking soda

1 teaspoon salt
1 teaspoon cinnamon
2 tablespoons butter
1/4 cup evaporated milk
1/2 cup sugar
1/2 teaspoon vanilla extract
1/2 cup shredded coconut
1/2 cup chopped nuts

Combine the boiling water, oats and 1/2 cup butter in a large bowl. Cover and let stand for 20 minutes. Add the brown sugar, 1 cup sugar, eggs, flour, baking soda, salt and cinnamon and mix well. Spoon into a nonstick 9×13-inch cake pan. Bake at 350 degrees for 35 minutes. Combine 2 tablespoons butter, evaporated milk, 1/2 cup sugar and vanilla in a mixing bowl and beat well. Stir in the coconut and nuts. Spread over the top of the hot cake. Broil for 2 minutes or until the top is brown.

YIELD: 15 SERVINGS

Captain James Lawrence

During the War of 1812, Lawrence commanded the USS *Hornet* in the capture of the HMS *Peacock*. Shortly thereafter he was promoted to captain of the frigate *Chesapeake*. In June of 1813, Lawrence accepted the challenge made by Philip Bowles Vere Broke, a captain in the Royal Navy, to a sea battle off the coast of Boston between the *Chesapeake* and the HMS *Shannon*. The *Chesapeake* was decisively defeated in less than an hour and Lawrence was mortally wounded. His dying phrase, "Don't give up the ship," is one of the United States Navy's most cherished traditions. Lawrence's words are the motto of the United States Navy and numerous ships have been named in his honor.

1814

General Andrew Jackson defeated Chief Weatherford in the Creek Indian War, forcing the Creeks to cede two-thirds of their vast territory (present day Georgia and Alabama) to the United States.

The British captured Washington, DC, and set fire to the Capitol Building, the White House, and the Navy Yard in retaliation for United States troops burning the capital in upper Canada.

All government buildings in Washington, DC, were burned except the patent office.

General Jackson captured Pensacola, Florida, and put New Orleans under martial law.

Popcorn Cake

4 quarts popped popcorn
2 cups unsalted peanuts
2 cups "M & M's" Plain Chocolate Candies
1 pound marshmallows
1 cup (2 sticks) butter

Combine the popcorn, peanuts and chocolate candies in a large bowl. Melt the marshmallows and butter in a saucepan over low heat, stirring constantly. Pour over the popcorn mixture and mix well with buttered hands. Press into a well-buttered tube pan. Let stand for 1 hour. Invert onto a serving plate and cut into small pieces.

YIELD: 16 SERVINGS

Eggnog Pound Cake

1 cup (2 sticks) butter or margarine,
   softened
1/2 cup shortening
3 cups sugar
6 eggs
3 cups flour
1 cup commercial eggnog
1 cup flaked coconut
1 teaspoon lemon extract
1 teaspoon vanilla extract
1/2 teaspoon coconut extract

Cream the butter and shortening in a mixing bowl until light and fluffy. Add the sugar gradually, beating constantly at medium speed. Add the eggs one at a time, beating well after each addition. Add the flour alternately with the eggnog, beating until blended after each addition and beginning and ending with the flour. Stir in the coconut and flavorings. Pour into a greased and floured 10-inch tube pan. Bake at 325 degrees for 1 1/2 hours or until a wooden pick inserted in the center comes out clean. Cool in the pan for 10 minutes. Remove from the pan to a wire rack to cool completely.

YIELD: 16 SERVINGS

Pound Cake

This old family recipe is delicious and requires no flavoring.

> 3 cups flour
> 1/2 teaspoon baking powder
> 1 1/2 cups (3 sticks) butter, softened
> 3 cups sugar
> 5 eggs
> 1 1/4 cups milk

Sift the flour and baking powder together. Cream the butter and sugar in a mixing bowl until light and fluffy. Add the eggs one at a time, beating well after each addition. Add the flour mixture and beat well. Add the milk and beat well. Pour into a greased and floured tube pan. Bake at 300 degrees for 1 1/2 hours.

YIELD: 16 SERVINGS

Note: You may also bake in three greased and floured 5×9-inch loaf pans. You may also add almond extract to taste for variety.

Williamsburg Pound Cake

> 2 cups (4 sticks) butter, softened
> 2 cups sugar
> 12 egg yolks, beaten
> 12 egg whites, stiffly beaten
> 3 1/2 cups flour, sifted
> Honey
> 8 ounces pitted dates
> 8 large almonds, skins removed

Cream the butter and sugar in a mixing bowl until light and fluffy. Add the egg yolks and beat well. Fold in the egg whites. Add the flour gradually, beating well after each addition. Pour into a well-greased tube pan filling to within 1 inch of the top. Bake at 350 degrees for 1 hour or until golden brown and the cake tests done. Cool in the pan. Remove to a serving plate. Brush the cake with honey. Arrange the dates and almonds decoratively over the cake.

YIELD: 16 SERVINGS

Just Desserts

1814

Congress increased the army to 63,000 regulars.

Commander MacDonough defeated the British fleet on Lake Champlain.

A convention was held in Montreal to arrange for an exchange of prisoners of war between the United States and England.

President Madison received a proposal for negotiations and accepted it.

A Treaty of Peace was signed with Great Britain at Ghent, Belgium, on December 24.

The "Star Spangled Banner" was written by Francis Scott Key by the light of artillery fire while he was detained by the British.

Andrew Jackson's Blackberry Jam Cake

Andrew Jackson had an inveterate fondness for blackberries. A great favorite of the holiday season in both Tennessee and Kentucky was jam cake, made with blackberry or dewberry jam.

3 cups flour
2 teaspoons baking powder
1 teaspoon baking soda
1/4 teaspoon salt
1 teaspoon allspice
1 teaspoon cinnamon
3/4 cup (1 1/2 sticks) butter or margarine, softened

1 cup sugar
3 eggs
1/2 cup sour milk or buttermilk
1 cup blackberry jam
White frosting

Sift the flour, baking powder, baking soda, salt, allspice and cinnamon together 3 times. Cream the butter and sugar in a large mixing bowl until light and fluffy. Add the eggs and beat well. Add the sifted flour mixture and sour milk alternately, beating well after each addition. Fold in the jam. Pour into 2 greased 8-inch round cake pans. Bake at 350 degrees for 45 minutes or until golden brown. Cool in the pans for 10 minutes. Invert onto wire racks to cool completely. Spread your favorite white frosting between the layers and over the top and side of the cake.

YIELD: 12 SERVINGS

Andrew Jackson

Andrew Jackson, born in South Carolina, was largely a self-taught man who became prominent in the political arena early in his career after he was admitted to the bar. He moved to Tennessee when it became a state and became its first United States representative in the House in 1769, its senator in 1797, and a judge on its Supreme Court in 1798. He established with his wife, Rachel, the Hermitage in Nashville, and was named major general of the Tennessee militia during the War of 1812. He led troops to defeat the Creek Indians at Horseshoe Bend and routed the British at the Battle of New Orleans. Later he invaded Florida and battled the Seminoles. He narrowly lost the bid for president to John Quincy Adams in 1824, but later won in 1828.

Lancaster Raisin Cake

This recipe was received from someone who had traveled to the Nebraska Territory in a covered wagon as a bride from Lancaster County, Pennsylvania. She lived in a sod house for several years and made friends with the Indians, which saved her life and that of her family several times. One Christmas she had nothing with which to provide the lavish spread of food which was the custom in her Pennsylvania family. So she used dried berries (which the Indians showed her), bear's fat for shortening, and dried herbs for spices.

2 cups boiling water	1 tablespoon cinnamon
1 pound raisins	1 teaspoon ground cloves
1 cup cold water	1 teaspoon nutmeg
1 tablespoon baking soda	4 cups flour
2 cups sugar	1/2 teaspoon salt
1/2 cup shortening	Vanilla extract to taste

Pour the boiling water over the raisins in a saucepan. Simmer for 15 minutes. Remove from the heat. Add the cold water. Let stand for 5 minutes. Stir in the baking soda. Add the remaining ingredients and mix well. Pour into a greased and floured bundt or tube pan. Place in the oven beside a small pan of cold water. Bake at 300 degrees for 1¹/4 hours. Cool in the pan for 15 minutes. Invert onto a wire rack to cool completely.

YIELD: 16 SERVINGS

Battle of New Orleans

Rum Cake

1¹/2 cups (3 sticks) margarine, softened
1 (16-ounce) package confectioners' sugar
3 cups cake flour

7 eggs
2 teaspoons rum or rum extract
Rum Glaze

Cream the margarine in a mixing bowl. Add the confectioners' sugar gradually, beating until light and fluffy. Add the cake flour alternately with the eggs, beating well after each addition. Stir in the rum. Pour into a greased and floured tube pan. Bake at 300 degrees for 1 hour and 20 minutes. Remove from the oven. Punch holes in the cake using an ice pick. Pour Rum Glaze in a fine stream over the hot cake. Let stand for 15 minutes. Remove the cake from the pan. The cake will have absorbed all of the glaze and will not be messy.

YIELD: 16 SERVINGS

Rum Glaze

1¹/2 cups sugar
¹/2 cup (1 stick) butter

¹/2 cup water
¹/2 cup white rum

Combine the sugar, butter and water in a saucepan. Bring to a boil. Boil for 3 minutes or until smooth, stirring constantly. Stir in the rum. Remove from the heat.

YIELD: ABOUT 3 CUPS

Commodore Oliver Hazard Perry
Oliver H. Perry was a United States naval officer who became famous for his heroism during the War of 1812. He received command of the Lake Erie naval fleet, which had been built in just nine months. The naval force won a great battle capturing six vessels of the British fleet. Upon his victory, Perry sent to General William Henry Harrison, the military commander in the west, the famous message, "We have met the enemy, and they are ours." For this victory, Perry was promoted to captain and received a gold medal and monetary rewards.

Cooked Chocolate Icing

1/2 cup (1 stick) butter or margarine
2 (1-ounce) squares unsweetened
   chocolate
2 cups sugar

Pinch of salt
1/2 cup milk
1 teaspoon vanilla extract

Melt the butter and chocolate in a saucepan. Add the sugar, salt and milk and mix well. Bring to a boil. Boil for 1 minute. Remove from the heat and cool. Add the vanilla. Beat for a few minutes or until of a spreadable consistency.

YIELD: ABOUT 3 CUPS

Never-Fail Caramel Icing

2 1/2 cups sugar
1 egg, lightly beaten
1/2 cup (1 stick) butter

3/4 cup milk
1 teaspoon vanilla extract
Cream

Caramelize 1/2 cup of the sugar in a cast-iron skillet over low heat, stirring constantly. Remove from the heat. Combine the remaining sugar, egg, butter and milk in a saucepan. Cook over low heat until the butter melts, stirring occasionally. Increase the heat to medium. Add the caramelized sugar. Cook to 238 degrees on a candy thermometer, soft-ball stage. Remove from the heat. Cool slightly. Add the vanilla. Beat until of a spreadable consistency, adding a small amount of cream if needed.

YIELD: ENOUGH TO FROST A 2-LAYER CAKE

Francis Scott Key

On September 13, 1814, young lawyer Francis Scott Key paced the decks of a captured American ship, watching the bombardment of Fort McHenry. He spent a restless night and the first thing he saw at dawn the next day was the American flag, still flying above the uncaptured fort. The commemorative poem he wrote was to become our national anthem.

Little Benne Cakes

Benne seeds (Sesamun indicum) *allegedly carry the secret of health and good luck. Southern cooks have long used these spicy seeds to enhance culinary delicacies. Little Benne Cakes were reported to have been one of Andrew Jackson's favorite confections.*

3 cups flour	*1/2 cup milk*
2 teaspoons baking powder	*3/4 cup (1 1/2 sticks) butter, softened*
1/2 teaspoon salt	*1/2 cup sugar*
1/2 teaspoon nutmeg	*Grated zest of 1 orange*
1 egg	*Benne Seed Glaze (below)*

Sift the flour, baking powder, salt and nutmeg together. Beat the egg and milk in a small bowl. Cream the butter and sugar in a mixing bowl until light and fluffy. Add the flour mixture alternately with the egg mixture, beating well after each addition. Add the orange zest and mix well. Roll a tablespoon of the dough at a time into a ball and arrange on a greased cookie sheet. Flatten each ball. Bake at 350 degrees for 10 minutes or until golden brown. Cool on a wire rack. Spread with Benne Seed Glaze.

YIELD: 3 DOZEN

Benne Seed Glaze

3/4 cup honey	*3 tablespoons benne seeds or sesame seeds,*
2 tablespoons butter	*toasted*

Combine the honey, butter and benne seeds in a saucepan. Cook to 250 to 268 degrees on a candy thermometer, hard-ball stage. Cool slightly. Spoon immediately over the cookies, working quickly as the glaze hardens quickly. Reheat over hot water if necessary, stirring to keep the benne seeds from rising to the top.

YIELD: 1 CUP

The Painting of George Washington

During the war, British Admiral Cockburn and his men entered the White House with destruction on their minds. Dolley Madison had set the table for dinner. The wine was already decanted. When the message came that the British were nearby, she fled, leaving the table set. As Dolley left, she rescued the painting of George Washington, taking it with her. Thanks to her quick thinking, generations of Americans have enjoyed this famous painting by Gilbert Stuart. (The British treated themselves to the dinner before burning the White House.)

Pralines

3/4 (12-ounce) can evaporated milk
2 cups sugar
1/2 teaspoon baking soda

1 teaspoon vanilla extract
3 cups pecan halves

Spread a dish towel on the countertop and cover with waxed paper. Sprinkle the waxed paper with salt. Combine the evaporated milk, sugar and baking soda in a deep saucepan and mix well. Cook over medium heat to 234 to 240 degrees on a candy thermometer, soft-ball stage. Remove from the heat. Add the vanilla and pecans and beat until creamy. Drop by spoonfuls onto the prepared waxed paper.

YIELD: 2 DOZEN

Pumpkin Chiffon Pie

1 envelope unflavored gelatin
1/4 cup cold water
2 egg whites
1/2 cup sugar
2 egg yolks, beaten
1 cup pumpkin
1/2 cup sugar

1/2 cup evaporated milk
1/2 teaspoon cinnamon
1/4 teaspoon ginger
1/4 teaspoon nutmeg
1/4 teaspoon salt
1 baked (9-inch) pie shell

Soften the gelatin in the cold water in a bowl. Beat the egg whites in a mixing bowl until foamy. Add 1/2 cup sugar gradually, beating until stiff peaks form. Combine the egg yolks, pumpkin, 1/2 cup sugar, evaporated milk, cinnamon, ginger, nutmeg and salt in a double boiler and mix well. Cook over hot water for 10 minutes or until thickened, stirring constantly. Add the gelatin mixture and mix until smooth. Remove from the heat to cool. Fold in the beaten egg whites. Pour into the baked pie shell. Chill until ready to serve.

YIELD: 8 SERVINGS

Note: You may stir chopped pecans into the filling or use as a garnish.

1815

The Battle of New Orleans was fought two weeks after the signing of the Treaty of Ghent, which officially ended the War of 1812 between the United States and Great Britain.

Congress declared war against Algeria for attacking American ships.

Captain Stephen Decatur left New York for Algiers with ten ships.

Captain Decatur captured the Algerian ships, *Mashouda* and *Estido*.

The United States Army was reduced to 10,000 men.

Apple Cheddar Crumble Pie

*3 cups thinly sliced peeled tart apples,
    such as Rhode Island Greening,
    Cortland or Granny Smith*
*3 cups thinly sliced peeled sweet apples,
    such as Rome Beauty or Jonathan*
1/4 cup fresh lemon juice
1 teaspoon finely grated lemon zest
3/4 cup sugar
2 tablespoons flour
1/2 teaspoon cinnamon
1/4 teaspoon salt
1/4 teaspoon freshly grated nutmeg
1/8 teaspoon allspice
Cheddar Cheese Crust (page 139)
1/3 cup flour
3 tablespoons brown sugar
*3 tablespoons cold unsalted butter,
    cut into 1/2-inch pieces*
1/2 cup shredded sharp Cheddar cheese

Combine the tart and sweet apples in a large bowl. Add the lemon juice and lemon zest and toss to coat. Mix the sugar, 2 tablespoons flour, cinnamon, salt, nutmeg and allspice in a small bowl. Sprinkle over the apples and toss to mix well. Spoon into the Cheddar Cheese Crust. Combine 1/3 cup flour, brown sugar, butter and Cheddar cheese in a bowl and toss to mix well. Sprinkle over the apple mixture. Bake at 425 degrees for 50 to 60 minutes or until the topping is golden brown. Cool on a wire rack for 30 minutes or longer before serving.

YIELD: 10 SERVINGS

Cheddar Cheese Crust

1 1/4 cups flour
1/2 teaspoon salt
1/8 teaspoon cayenne pepper
1/2 cup (1 stick) unsalted butter, sliced
3/4 cup shredded sharp Cheddar cheese
3 or 4 tablespoons cold water

Combine the flour, salt and cayenne pepper in a large bowl and mix well. Cut in the butter until crumbly. Add the Cheddar cheese and toss to mix well. Add the cold water a tablespoon at a time, mixing to form a rough dough. Shape the dough into a ball and flatten into a disk 3/4 inch thick. Wrap tightly in plastic wrap and chill for 30 minutes. Roll the dough on a lightly floured surface into an 11-inch circle, 1/4 inch thick. Fit into a 9-inch pie plate, turning the overhanging dough under to form an edge along the top of the pie plate. Crimp the edges. Chill for 30 minutes. Line the prepared pie shell with parchment paper and fill with pie weights or dried beans. Bake at 425 degrees for 15 minutes or until the crust is light brown. Cool on a wire rack. Remove the pie weights.

YIELD: 1 PIECRUST

Bear Bryant's Fudge Pie

1/2 cup (1 stick) butter
2 ounces unsweetened chocolate
1 cup sugar
1/4 cup flour
Pinch of salt
2 eggs, lightly beaten
1 tablespoon vanilla extract

Melt the butter and chocolate in a double boiler over hot water. Remove from the heat. Add the sugar, flour, salt and eggs and stir to mix well. Stir in the vanilla. Pour into a lightly greased pie plate. Place in an oven preheated to 375 degrees. Reduce the oven temperature to 325 degrees. Bake for 30 minutes. Serve warm with ice cream.

YIELD: 8 SERVINGS

1815

General Jackson was fined $1,000 for contempt of court in New Orleans after refusing to honor a writ of habeas corpus.

The estimated cost of the war with England came to $200 million.

The United States signed treaties with Indians who were allied with the British during the war.

In gratitude for his help at the Battle of New Orleans, President Madison pardoned pirate Jean Lafitte.

The government raised funds by taxing watches, hats, caps, and boots.

Frosty Lemon Pie

3/4 cup sugar
1/3 cup lemon juice
1/4 cup (1/2 stick) butter or margarine
Dash of salt

3 eggs, beaten
2 pints vanilla ice cream, softened
1 (9-inch) graham cracker pie shell

Combine the sugar, lemon juice, butter and salt in a double boiler. Cook over boiling water until the sugar is dissolved and the butter is melted, stirring constantly. Add a small amount of the hot mixture to the beaten eggs in a bowl. Stir the eggs into the hot mixture. Cook until thickened, stirring constantly. Do not boil. Remove from the heat. Chill until completely cool.

Spread 1/2 of the ice cream in the pie shell. Freeze for 1 hour or until firm. Cover with 1/2 of the chilled lemon mixture. Freeze for 1 hour or until firm. Repeat the layers with the remaining ice cream and lemon mixture. Freeze, covered, for 3 to 12 hours. Remove from the freezer 10 minutes before serving. Garnish with whipped topping and lemon zest.

YIELD: 8 SERVINGS

Note: You may store for several days in the freezer.

Commodore Joshua Barney

Joshua Barney was an American naval officer and hero, well known for his feats of daring during the Revolutionary War. In the War of 1812, he also engaged in large scale privateering. In July of 1814, he was given the task of checking the British advance up the Chesapeake Bay. For several weeks, he slowed the drive trying to prevent the British destruction of Washington DC. In the ensuing battle on August 24, the American lines were broken and Barney with his men, heroically stayed behind to cover the retreat. Their gallant defense failed and Barney was wounded and captured.

Key Lime Pie

1¹/4 cups graham cracker crumbs
3 tablespoons sugar
5 tablespoons unsalted butter, melted
4 teaspoons grated lime zest
4 egg yolks
1 (14-ounce) can sweetened condensed
  milk

¹/2 cup strained lime juice
³/4 cup whipping cream, chilled
¹/4 cup confectioners' sugar
¹/2 lime, thinly sliced
Sugar

Mix the graham cracker crumbs and 3 tablespoons sugar in a bowl. Add the butter and stir with a fork until blended. Press into a 9-inch pie plate to cover the bottom and side. Bake at 325 degrees for 15 minutes. Cool on a wire rack for 20 minutes.

Beat the lime zest and egg yolks in a mixing bowl until the mixture is tinted green. Add the condensed milk and beat well. Add the lime juice and beat well. Let stand at room temperature to thicken. Pour into the cooled crust. Bake at 325 degrees for 15 to 17 minutes or until set. Remove to a wire rack to cool to room temperature. Chill, covered with oiled plastic wrap, for 3 to 24 hours.

Beat the whipping cream in a chilled mixing bowl with chilled beaters until soft peaks form. Add the confectioners' sugar 1 tablespoon at a time, beating until stiff peaks form. Spread or decoratively pipe over the filling. Dip the lime slices in sugar. Arrange decoratively over the pie.

YIELD: 8 SERVINGS

Note: You may tint the filling with a couple of drops of green food coloring.

Major General Samuel Smith
Well known for his service during the American Revolution, the threat of war with France and England in 1794 led to Samuel Smith's appointment as brigadier general of the militia of Baltimore. He played a vital role in the defense of Baltimore during the War of 1812. He commanded the Army of Baltimore volunteers and was largely responsible for reinforcing Fort McHenry, which led to a retreat by the British.

Mile-High Peanut Butter Pie

1 1/2 cups Oreo cookie crumbs
2 tablespoons sugar
2 tablespoons unsalted butter, melted
12 ounces cream cheese, softened
1 1/2 cups creamy peanut butter
1 1/2 cups confectioners' sugar
3 tablespoons unsalted butter, softened

1 tablespoon vanilla extract
3/4 cup whipping cream, chilled
8 ounces bittersweet chocolate, chopped
1 tablespoon vegetable oil
2 cups whipping cream, chilled
1/4 cup confectioners' sugar

Mix the cookie crumbs, sugar and 2 tablespoons butter in a bowl until blended. Press evenly in a 9-inch pie plate, spreading over the bottom and up the side to the rim. Bake at 350 degrees on the lower oven rack for 10 minutes. Remove to a wire rack to cool.

Beat the cream cheese in a mixing bowl until light and fluffy. Add the peanut butter and mix well. Add 1 1/2 cups confectioners' sugar, 3 tablespoons butter and the vanilla and beat until smooth and fluffy. Beat 3/4 cup whipping cream in a mixing bowl until soft peaks form. Fold 1/3 of the whipped cream into the cream cheese mixture. Fold in the remaining whipped cream. Spoon into the cooled piecrust, mounding slightly in the center. Chill in the refrigerator.

Melt the chocolate in a double boiler over low heat. Remove from the heat and cool to lukewarm. Stir in the oil. Beat 2 cups whipping cream and 1/4 cup confectioners' sugar in a mixing bowl until soft peaks form. Add the chocolate mixture and beat just until combined and stiff. Spread over the chilled pie, mounding as high as possible in the center. Chill until ready to serve. Garnish with chocolate curls.

YIELD: 8 SERVINGS

Note: You may use a purchased chocolate pie shell. Do not use fresh ground or old-fashioned peanut butter in this recipe.

James Biddle

James Biddle, a United States naval officer and diplomat, became a midshipman in 1800. At the beginning of the War of 1812 he was first lieutenant on the *Wasp*; he later commanded the sloop *Hornet*. He took formal possession of the Oregon Territory for the United States in 1818 and later negotiated the first treaty between the United States and China.

Classic Pecan Pie

3 cups flour
1 teaspoon baking powder
¹/4 teaspoon salt
1 cup shortening
2 eggs
1 tablespoon vinegar
1 tablespoon water

3 eggs
1 cup sugar
1 cup light or dark corn syrup
2 tablespoons margarine, melted
1 teaspoon vanilla extract
1¹/2 cups pecan halves

Mix the flour, baking powder and salt in a bowl. Cut in the shortening until crumbly. Beat 2 eggs, the vinegar and water in a mixing bowl until blended. Add to the flour mixture and stir to form a ball. Roll into a circle on a lightly floured surface. Fit into a 9-inch pie plate, trimming and fluting the edge.

Beat 3 eggs lightly in a mixing bowl. Add the sugar, corn syrup, margarine and vanilla and blend well. Stir in the pecans. Pour into the prepared pie shell. Bake at 350 degrees for 50 to 55 minutes or until a knife inserted halfway between the center and the edge comes out clean. Cool on a wire rack.

YIELD: 8 SERVINGS

Brigadier General John Coffee
John Coffee played a significant role in Andrew Jackson's campaign against the Creek Indians in Alabama. While he was serving as brigadier general of Tennessee volunteers they were instrumental in all of Jackson's battle victories including Horseshoe Bend. Coffee and his men participated in the invasion of Spanish Florida, the capture of Pensacola, and the victory in New Orleans. He remained one of Jackson's most trusted friends and advisors.

The Legacy

MRS. DEE WALLACE WARD, JR. TEA

PRESIDENTS' BUFFET

THE USD 1812 HOUSE
1461 RHODE ISLAND AVENUE NW
WASHINGTON, DC

The National Society United States Daughters of 1812 has its
headquarters in this house. The Society has many purposes that are patriotic,
historic, and educational. Preservation of our nation's history during the
time period 1784–1815 is of primary concern to our members.

The house not only serves as National Headquarters, but houses a
library and museum as well. The recent purchase of the house next door
will allow the expansion of these facilities.

Proceeds from the sale of *Savor the Spirit* cookbooks will
benefit the House Restoration Fund to help finance the renovations.

COOKBOOK COMMITTEE
ALABAMA SOCIETY USD OF 1812

Alabama Society
United States Daughters of 1812
Requests your presence
At a tea honoring
MRS. DEE WALLACE WARD, JR.
President
National Society
United States Daughters of 1812
1461 Rhode Island Avenue NW
Washington, DC
April 7, 2002

Mrs. Dee Wallace Ward, Jr. Tea

Chicken Salad Cups

Tomato Aspic Appetizers

Pimento Cheese Sandwiches

Ham Spread Sandwiches

Toasted Pecans

Cheese Straws

Snickerdoodles

Sugar Cookies

Chocolate Squares

Punch and Tea

Tomato Aspic Appetizer

Mayonnaise
2 cups tomato juice
1 (3-ounce) package lemon gelatin
1 teaspoon unflavored gelatin
$1/2$ teaspoon bottled onion juice

$1/2$ teaspoon salt
$1^1/2$ cups finely chopped celery
3 ounces cream cheese, softened
2 tablespoons mayonnaise
$1/4$ cup pecans, toasted, chopped

Wash three plastic egg cartons and pat dry. Brush the inside of the cups with mayonnaise. Heat the tomato juice in a saucepan. Add the lemon gelatin and unflavored gelatin. Heat until dissolved, stirring constantly. Add the onion juice, salt and celery. Spoon into the prepared cups. Beat the cream cheese and 2 tablespoons mayonnaise in a small mixing bowl until smooth and creamy. Stir in the pecans. Spoon into the center of each cup. Chill in the refrigerator until firm. Unmold using a teaspoon and serve on butter crackers.

YIELD: ABOUT 3 DOZEN

Tea

Drinking tea in England in the 1600s was prescribed to alleviate many health problems, such as headaches and kidney stones. Gradually, taking tea became more of a social custom and was emulated by eighteenth century American colonists. However, British taxes on tea led to a boycott by the colonists and eventually the famous Boston Tea Party of 1773. Americans began to drink tea again in 1776. By the mid-1800s, tea served as a meal was established. Proper tea accoutrements were extremely important, as was the manner in which tea was served.

Miniature Quiches

1 (12-ounce) package refrigerated
 butterflake dinner rolls
1 (4-ounce) can shrimp, drained
1 egg, beaten
1/2 cup light cream or evaporated milk

1 tablespoon brandy
1/2 teaspoon salt
Dash of pepper
1 1/2 ounces Gruyère cheese, Swiss cheese
 or Cheddar cheese

Separate each roll into halves. Press each half into a greased 1 3/4-inch muffin cup to form a shell. Arrange 1 shrimp in each shell. Combine the egg, cream, brandy, salt and pepper in a bowl and mix well. Spoon about 2 teaspoonfuls into each shell. Cut the Gruyère cheese into 24 small triangles. Arrange over the top of each shell. Bake at 375 degrees for 20 minutes or until golden brown. Serve warm.

YIELD: 2 DOZEN

Asparagus Roll-Ups

25 slices white bread
8 ounces cream cheese, softened
3 ounces bleu cheese, crumbled
1 egg

White pepper to taste
25 fresh asparagus spears, blanched
1 1/2 cups (3 sticks) butter, melted

Trim the crusts from the bread and flatten with a rolling pin. Combine the cream cheese, bleu cheese and egg in a small mixing bowl and beat until smooth. Season with white pepper. Spread over the flattened bread slices. Arrange an asparagus spear on one side of each slice, trimming the stem if necessary. Roll up tightly to enclose the asparagus. Dip roll-ups in the melted butter and arrange on a baking sheet. Freeze, covered, until ready to serve. To serve, cut the frozen roll-ups into thirds and arrange on baking sheets. Bake at 400 degrees for 15 minutes or until golden brown. Serve hot.

YIELD: 25 SERVINGS

Chicken Salad in Shells

4 boneless skinless chicken breasts, cooked,
  finely chopped
6 hard-cooked eggs, finely chopped
  (optional)
4 or 5 ribs celery, finely chopped
1/2 cup slivered almonds, toasted

Mayonnaise, Tabasco sauce and lemon
  juice to taste
Salt and pepper to taste
Cream Cheese Miniature Pastry Shells
  (below)
75 pecan halves, toasted

Combine the chicken, eggs, celery, almonds, mayonnaise, Tabasco sauce, lemon juice, salt and pepper in a large bowl and mix well. Chill, covered, until ready to serve. To serve, fill Cream Cheese Miniature Pastry Shells with the chicken salad. Top each with a toasted pecan half.

YIELD: 75 SERVINGS

Cream Cheese Miniature Pastry Shells

1 cup (2 sticks) margarine, softened
8 ounces cream cheese, softened

2 1/2 cups flour
1 teaspoon salt

Cream the margarine and cream cheese in a mixing bowl until light and fluffy. Blend in the flour and salt. Press into miniature muffin cups. Bake at 350 degrees until light brown.

YIELD: 75 SERVINGS

The Pleasure of Tea

Afternoon teas first became popular and fashionable in Victorian times. Although it was only considered as light refreshment between lunch and dinner, afternoon tea was quite a serious occasion, and ladies were renowned for their prowess at teamaking. Usually served between the hours of four and five o'clock, the taste and refinement of the hostess would be judged by the quality and manner in which she served her afternoon tea. There would be a selection of dainty sandwiches, fancy biscuits, which had to be dry in texture so as not to soil the guests' fingers, and various delicious cakes. All were presented and served on the finest and most delicate of bone china, with tiny silver teaspoons and tea served from a silver teapot.

Almond Chicken Tea Sandwiches

3 boneless skinless chicken breasts
1 small onion
1 rib celery
1 carrot
Salt to taste

1/2 cup slivered blanched almonds, chopped
1/2 cup finely chopped celery
1/2 cup mayonnaise
1 loaf sliced white or whole wheat bread,
  crusts trimmed

Combine the chicken, onion, celery, carrot and salt in a saucepan. Cover with water. Bring to a boil and reduce the heat. Simmer, covered, until the chicken is cooked through. Drain the chicken, discarding the cooking vegetables. Let stand until cool. Chop the chicken. Combine the chicken, almonds, celery and mayonnaise in a bowl and mix well. Season with salt. Spread over 1/2 of the bread slices. Top with the remaining bread slices. Cut the sandwiches into triangles or strips.

YIELD: 40 SERVINGS

Smoked Chicken Salad Sandwiches

8 ounces cooked smoked chicken or turkey,
  finely chopped
1 rib celery, thinly sliced
1/2 Red Delicious apple, chopped
1/2 cup mayonnaise
1 teaspoon fresh thyme, or 1/2 teaspoon
  dried thyme

Pepper to taste
1 small cucumber, thinly sliced
12 slices whole-grain bread, toasted
Alfalfa sprouts

Combine the chicken, celery, apple, mayonnaise, thyme and pepper in a bowl and mix well. Arrange the cucumber slices on 1/2 of the bread slices. Spread with the chicken mixture. Arrange the alfalfa sprouts over the chicken mixture. Top with the remaining bread slices. Cut each sandwich into quarters.

YIELD: 24 SERVINGS

Cream Cheese, Celery and Walnut Sandwiches

8 ounces cream cheese, softened
1/2 cup very finely chopped celery
   hearts

1/2 cup very finely chopped walnuts
1 loaf sliced white or whole wheat bread,
   crusts trimmed

Beat the cream cheese in a mixing bowl until smooth. Add the celery and walnuts and mix well. Spread the cream cheese mixture over 1/2 of the bread slices. Top with the remaining bread slices. Cut into rectangles or triangles.

YIELD: 20 SERVINGS

Cucumber Dill Sandwiches

8 ounces cream cheese, softened
1 envelope Italian salad dressing mix
2 teaspoons milk

1 cucumber
1 loaf party rye bread
Dillweed or chopped chives

Combine the cream cheese, salad dressing mix and milk in a mixing bowl and beat until smooth. Let stand for 30 minutes to enhance the flavor. Cut the cucumber into very thin slices. Cut the bread into 1 1/2-inch circles. Spread the cream cheese mixture on the bread rounds. Top with the cucumbers. Sprinkle with dillweed. Chill, covered, until ready to serve.

YIELD: 40 SERVINGS

The Benefits of Tea

- Raise a cup of tea as a toast to good health!
- Tea drinking is a delightful habit to cultivate.
- Not only does the ceremony of teatime lift spirits, the health benefits are yours to enjoy as well!
- Tea helps relieve fatigue, lift the spirits, and stimulate the mind.
- A cup of tea contains zero calories. (Add forty calories if served with milk and sugar.)

Egg Salad Sandwiches

2 hard-cooked eggs, chopped
1/2 cup mayonnaise
1 teaspoon prepared mustard
1 teaspoon sweet pickle relish

1 teaspoon fresh chives, finely chopped
Salt to taste
1 loaf sliced white or whole wheat bread,
 crusts trimmed

Combine the eggs, mayonnaise, mustard, pickle relish, chives and salt in a bowl and mix well. Spread the mixture over 1/2 of the bread slices. Top with the remaining bread slices. Cut the sandwiches into desired shapes.

YIELD: 20 SERVINGS

Ham Sandwich Spread

1 cup (1-inch) cubed cooked ham
2 (2-inch) sweet pickles, sliced
1 thin slice small onion

1 carrot, sliced
1/2 cup mayonnaise

Process the ham 1/2 cup at a time, in a blender or food processor until grated. Spoon into a bowl. Process the pickles, onion and carrot in a blender or food processor until grated. Add to the ham and mix well. Stir in the mayonnaise. Chill, covered, until ready to serve.

YIELD: 1 1/2 CUPS

Iced Tea

In 1904, visitors to the Louisiana Purchase Exposition in St. Louis sweltered in a heat wave and declined the hot brew offered by Indian tea growers. An Englishman named Richard Blechynded, who represented the tea growers, tried pouring the tea over ice in order to please his visitors. The result was iced tea, which now accounts for 80 percent of the tea consumed in the United States.

Parsley Bacon Sandwiches

2 bunches fresh parsley, chopped
1 pound bacon, cooked, drained,
   crumbled
Mayonnaise
Worcestershire sauce

Butter, softened
Garlic powder to taste
1 loaf sliced fresh sandwich bread,
   crusts trimmed

Combine the parsley and bacon in a bowl and toss to mix. Add enough mayonnaise and Worcestershire sauce to make of a spreading consistency. Beat the butter and garlic powder in a mixing bowl until smooth and creamy. Roll the bread slices lightly with a rolling pin. Spread with the garlic butter. Spread the parsley mixture over the garlic butter. Cut into strips or triangles.

YIELD: 9 DOZEN

Note: May be frozen.

Pimento Cheese Spread

8 ounces cream cheese, softened
12 ounces shredded Cheddar cheese
1 (7-ounce) jar sliced pimentos, drained

Juice from a bottle of stuffed olives
Salt and Tabasco sauce to taste
Mayonnaise

Combine the cream cheese and Cheddar cheese in a bowl and mix well. Add the pimentos, olive juice, salt and Tabasco sauce and mix well. Add enough mayonnaise to make of a spreading consistency.

YIELD: ABOUT 4 CUPS

Cheese Straws

2 cups sifted flour
1/4 teaspoon cayenne pepper
1/2 teaspoon salt
1/8 teaspoon ground cloves

1/8 teaspoon grated nutmeg
1 pound sharp New York cheese, grated
1/2 cup (1 stick) butter or margarine,
  softened

Sift the flour, cayenne pepper, salt, cloves and nutmeg together. Mix the cheese and butter in a large bowl to form a smooth paste using your hands. Sprinkle the flour mixture gradually over the cheese mixture, kneading to form a pliable dough. Spoon the dough into a cookie press fitted with a star tip. Press into long strips on a nonstick baking sheet. Cut into 2-inch lengths. Sprinkle lightly with salt to taste. Bake at 375 to 400 degrees for 10 minutes or until golden brown. Cool on a wire rack. Store between layers of waxed paper in a tightly covered container.

YIELD: ABOUT 7 DOZEN

Salted Pecans

1 teaspoon salt
1/4 cup water

4 cups pecan halves
1 tablespoon margarine, melted

Dissolve the salt in the water in a bowl. Spread the pecans in a baking pan. Pour the salt water over the pecans. Bake at 275 degrees for 30 to 40 minutes or until the pecans are dry, stirring occasionally. Pour the melted margarine over the pecans and stir to coat. Spread on waxed paper. Let stand until dry.

YIELD: 4 CUPS

White House Cheese

For his last reception, President Andrew Jackson invited the public to share the 1,400-pound cheese he had received from New York dairymen. Measuring three feet thick and four feet in diameter, the cheese had been kept in the White House cellar for a year to age and ripen. The result was described by some as "an evil-smelling horror." Nonetheless, shops and offices declared a holiday and 10,000 cheese lovers marched on—-or should we say stormed—-the White House. By the time the last guest had gone, the cheese stand was empty, and the cheese had been transferred to the carpets, walls, drapes, and furniture. The scent remained in the East Room for a month.

Scones

2 cups flour
1 tablespoon baking powder
1/4 teaspoon salt
1/4 cup sugar
6 tablespoons butter

2 eggs, beaten
1/3 cup cream, milk or half-and-half
Milk
Sugar

Mix the flour, baking powder, salt and 1/4 cup sugar in a bowl. Cut in the butter until crumbly. Combine the eggs and cream in a bowl and beat until blended. Add to the flour mixture and stir just until moistened. Do not mix for too long or the scones will be tough. Divide the dough into 2 equal portions. Shape each portion into an 8-inch round on a greased baking sheet. Cut each round into 8 wedges with a sharp knife. Brush with milk and sprinkle with sugar. Bake at 400 degrees for 10 to 15 minutes or until the scones are golden brown. Serve with Mock Devonshire Cream (below), Lemon Curd or Strawberry Jam (page 157).

YIELD: 16 SERVINGS

Mock Devonshire Cream

8 ounces cream cheese, softened
2 tablespoons confectioners' sugar

1/2 cup sour cream

Beat the cream cheese and confectioners' sugar in a mixing bowl until smooth. Add the sour cream and beat until blended. Serve with scones.

YIELD: 1 1/2 CUPS

Scones

Like giant, flaky, slightly sweet biscuits, scones are the staple of a proper tea. The proper pronunciation of "scone" rhymes with "lawn," not "cone." Traditionally, scones are served with clotted cream or Devonshire cream instead of butter. You can also add fruit preserves, lemon curd, or other delicious toppings. Fresh strawberries on the side taste wonderful, too.

Lemon Curd

3 large eggs
Grated zest of 3 large lemons
Juice of 3 large lemons

6 tablespoons butter
1 cup plus 3 tablespoons sugar

Beat the eggs lightly in a double boiler. Add the lemon zest, lemon juice, butter and sugar. Heat over boiling water until the butter melts, stirring constantly. Cook for 5 to 10 minutes longer, stirring constantly. Serve with scones or use as a filling in small tart shells.

YIELD: ABOUT 2 CUPS

Note: To store, ladle into hot sterilized jars, leaving 1/2 inch headspace; seal with 2-piece lids. Process in a boiling water bath for 10 minutes.

Strawberry Jam

4 to 6 pints strawberries
3 cups sugar

2 teaspoons fresh lemon juice

Rinse the strawberries and pat dry. Remove and discard the hulls from the strawberries. Purée enough strawberries in a food processor to equal 4 cups. Pour into a large nonaluminum saucepan. Stir in the sugar and lemon juice. Bring to a boil and reduce the heat to low. Simmer for 9 to 15 minutes or until thickened, stirring frequently with a stainless steel spoon. Remove from the heat. Cool to room temperature. Pour into a large bowl. Chill, covered, for 2 to 3 hours. Spoon into a large nonaluminum saucepan. Simmer for 9 to 15 minutes or until thickened. Ladle into eight 8-ounce hot sterilized jars, leaving 1/2 inch headspace; seal with 2-piece lids. Process in a boiling water bath for 10 minutes.

YIELD: EIGHT (8-OUNCE) JARS

Apricot Balls

1 1/2 cups dried apricots, ground
2 cups shredded coconut

2/3 cup sweetened condensed milk
Confectioners' sugar

Mix the apricots and coconut in a bowl. Add the condensed milk and mix well. Shape into balls. Roll in confectioners' sugar and arrange on a large tray. Let stand until firm. Store in paper candy cups in an airtight container in the refrigerator.

YIELD: 32 BALLS

Cheese Date Tarts

1 cup grated sharp New York Cheddar
  cheese, softened
1/2 cup (1 stick) butter, softened
1 1/3 cups flour
1/4 teaspoon salt

1 (16-ounce) package seedless dates,
  finely chopped
1/2 cup packed brown sugar
2 or 3 tablespoons water

Combine the cheese and butter in a bowl and mix well. Add the flour and salt and mix well. Chill, covered, in the refrigerator. Combine the dates, brown sugar and water in a saucepan and mix well. Cook until thickened, stirring constantly. Remove from the heat. Roll the pastry a small amount at a time on a lightly floured surface. Cut into circles with a small biscuit cutter. Spread each circle with the date filling. Fold over and prick the edge with a fork to seal. Arrange on a baking sheet. Bake at 350 degrees for 10 minutes.

YIELD: 30 SERVINGS

Note: May be frozen. Thaw completely and heat in a warm oven before serving.

Scotch Shortbread

1/2 cup (1 stick) or more butter, softened   *1 1/2 cups flour*
1/4 cup sugar

Cream the butter and sugar in a mixing bowl until light and fluffy. Stir in the flour gradually, adding an additional 1 to 2 tablespoons butter if the dough is crumbly. Press into a greased baking pan. Mark into squares and prick with a fork. Bake at 325 degrees for 30 to 35 minutes or until light golden brown.

YIELD: 1 1/3 DOZEN

Sugar Cookies

1 cup (2 sticks) margarine, softened   *1 teaspoon cream of tartar*
1 cup sugar   *1 teaspoon baking soda*
1 cup confectioners' sugar   *1 teaspoon salt*
2 eggs   *4 1/2 cups flour*
1 cup vegetable oil   *Sugar*
1 teaspoon vanilla, orange or lemon
  extract

Combine the margarine, 1 cup sugar, confectioners' sugar, eggs, oil, vanilla, cream of tartar, baking soda and salt in a mixing bowl. Beat at low speed until smooth. Add the flour and mix well. Shape into small balls. Arrange on a cookie sheet. Press with a glass dipped in sugar to flatten. Bake at 350 degrees for 5 to 6 minutes or until golden brown. Remove to a wire rack to cool.

YIELD: 6 TO 7 DOZEN

Tea Bags

Tea bags were invented quite by accident in 1904 by a New York tea merchant. Instead of sending samples of tea to his customers in standard tea tins, the innovative merchant came up with the idea of packaging them in handsewn silk bags. Soon he was overwhelmed with orders for tea in bags.

Lavender Tea Cookies

1 cup (2 sticks) unsalted butter, softened
2/3 cup minus 1 tablespoon superfine
  sugar
1 egg, beaten

1 cup plus 3 tablespoons self-rising flour
1 tablespoon fresh lavender flowers
1/2 teaspoon almond extract

Beat the butter and sugar in a mixing bowl until light and fluffy. Add the egg and beat well. Stir in the self-rising flour, lavender flowers and almond flavoring. Drop by teaspoonfuls 2 inches apart onto a cookie sheet lined with parchment paper. Bake at 350 degrees for 10 to 15 minutes or until pale golden brown. Cool on waxed paper until firm. Store in an airtight container.

YIELD: 2 1/2 DOZEN

Tea Cakes

4 1/2 cups flour
1 teaspoon baking soda
1 teaspoon baking powder
1 teaspoon cream of tartar
1 cup sugar
1 cup (2 sticks) margarine, softened

1 cup vegetable oil
2 eggs
1 tablespoon vanilla extract
1 teaspoon lemon extract
Confectioners' sugar

Mix the flour, baking soda, baking powder and cream of tartar in a bowl. Combine the sugar, margarine, oil and eggs in a mixing bowl and beat until creamy. Stir in the flavorings. Add the flour mixture and mix well. Drop by scant teaspoonfuls 2 inches apart onto an ungreased cookie sheet. Bake at 325 degrees for 10 minutes or until golden brown. Cool slightly. Roll in or sprinkle with confectioners' sugar.

YIELD: ABOUT 4 DOZEN

Preparing Tea

To prepare your tea in the proper way, steep instead of boiling it. Tea leaves release their flavor in hot water, and the taste is more pleasant in the beverage that has been steeped. The hotter the water, the faster the tea will steep. Three to five minutes is sufficient steeping time for most teas. The term "the agony of the leaves" refers to the process of the leaves uncurling when the hot water is poured over them.

Grandma's Tea Cakes

3 to 4 cups flour
1 teaspoon baking soda
3 eggs
2 cups packed brown sugar

1 cup (2 sticks) butter, melted
Cinnamon or nutmeg to taste
Raisins

Sift the flour and baking soda together. Beat the eggs in a mixing bowl until frothy. Add the brown sugar, butter and cinnamon and mix well. Stir in enough of the flour mixture to make a soft dough, adding additional flour if needed. Roll into a thin circle on a lightly floured surface. Cut with a round cookie cutter. Arrange the raisins on the top of each circle to make a face complete with eyes, nose and smile; press into the dough. Arrange on a nonstick cookie sheet. Bake at 375 to 400 degrees until golden brown. Remove to a wire rack to cool.

YIELD: 3 TO 4 DOZEN

Owen Family Tea Cakes

This is a recipe from the family of Thomas Hennington Owen, who built his plantation home in 1833 in Jonesboro, Alabama, in Jefferson County. The home is maintained as a museum by the West Jefferson County Historical Society. The Owens were pioneers of Alabama arriving here by 1816.

1 cup (2 sticks) butter, softened
1 cup sugar
2 eggs

1 teaspoon vanilla extract
1/2 teaspoon baking powder
3 cups (about) flour

Beat the butter and sugar in a mixing bowl until light and fluffy. Add the eggs and vanilla and beat well. Stir in the baking powder and enough flour to form a stiff dough. The dough will be sticky. Roll into a circle on waxed paper. Cut into circles with a round cookie cutter. Lift each circle with a spatula and arrange on a greased cookie sheet. Bake at 375 degrees for 10 minutes. Remove to a wire rack to cool.

YIELD: 3 DOZEN

Tea

Party Punch

4 cups strong brewed tea
4 cups brewed mint tea
1 teaspoon whole cloves
4 cups pineapple juice
4 cups apple juice

4 cups orange juice
1/2 cup lemon juice
2 liters ginger ale
1 fifth light rum

Combine the brewed teas and cloves in a large container and mix well. Let stand until cool. Add the pineapple juice, apple juice, orange juice and lemon juice and mix well. Stir in the ginger ale and light rum. Serve over ice in glasses. Garnish with mint and fruit slices.

YIELD: 30 SERVINGS

Frosted Fruit Shrub

3 cups cranberry juice
3/4 cup apple juice

1 pint raspberry sherbet

Combine the cranberry juice and apple juice in a pitcher and mix well. Chill in the refrigerator. Pour into serving glasses. Top each with a scoop of raspberry sherbet and stir once or twice. Garnish with mint sprigs.

YIELD: 6 SERVINGS

Note: May use pineapple and orange juice and serve with orange sherbet.

Shrubs

Shrubs are drinks made with a fruit base. They are part of the heritage of colonial America. There seems to be little rationale for the name (although "shrub" may derive from the Arabic *shurb*, meaning drink). Early settlers in the South soon discovered the advantages of the wild blackberry in both food and drink. The blackberry shrub was a special favorite of Andrew Jackson.

Iced Tea with Mint

1 cup sugar
4 cups water
8 sprigs of fresh mint

8 small tea bags
1/2 cup lemon juice
4 cups cold water

Bring the sugar and 4 cups water to a boil in a saucepan and reduce the heat. Simmer for 10 minutes. Add the mint and tea bags. Steep for 10 minutes. Remove and discard the mint and tea bags. Stir in the lemon juice and 4 cups cold water. Serve over ice in glasses.

YIELD: 8 SERVINGS

Note: May make in large quantities the day before serving.

Special Tea

8 cups water
1 cup sugar
6 tea bags

10 whole cloves
1/4 cup lemon juice
1 cup orange juice

Bring the water and sugar to a boil in a saucepan. Remove from the heat. Add the tea bags and cloves. Let stand for 5 minutes. Remove and discard the tea bags and cloves. Add the lemon juice and orange juice and mix well.

YIELD: 8 SERVINGS

Spiced Tea

2 cups Tang
2 cups sugar
1 cup instant tea mix

1 envelope lemonade mix
1 teaspoon cinnamon
1 teaspoon ground cloves

Mix the Tang, sugar, instant tea mix, lemonade mix, cinnamon and cloves in a bowl. Store in an airtight container. To serve, mix about 2 tablespoons of the mixture in 1 cup hot water in a cup.

YIELD: ABOUT 30 SERVINGS

Presidents' Buffet

Rosalynn Carter's Plains Special Cheese Ring

President Monroe's Quaking Jelly

Nancy Reagan's Baja California Chicken

The Hermitage's Turkey Hash

Mrs. Lyndon B. Johnson's Spoon Bread

Betty Ford's Blue Banana Bread

Mrs. Lincoln's White Cake

Jacqueline Kennedy's Lace Cookies

Rosalynn Carter's Plains Special Cheese Ring

1 pound grated sharp cheese
1 cup finely chopped nuts
1 small onion, finely grated

1 cup mayonnaise
Cayenne pepper and black pepper to taste
Strawberry preserves

Combine the cheese, nuts, onion and mayonnaise in a bowl and mix well. Season with cayenne pepper and black pepper. Pack into a lightly greased 5- or 6-cup ring mold. Chill for 3 to 12 hours or until firm. To serve, unmold onto a serving plate. Fill the center with strawberry preserves. Serve with crackers.

YIELD: 12 SERVINGS

President Monroe's Quaking Jelly

2 envelopes unflavored gelatin
1/2 cup cold water
2 cups tomato juice
2 cups chicken broth
1 teaspoon grated lemon zest
1 teaspoon grated onion
2 teaspoons chopped fresh parsley

2 tablespoons dry sherry
1 tablespoon lemon juice
Salt to taste
Dash of white pepper
1 cup sour cream
3 tablespoons chopped fresh chives

Combine the gelatin and cold water in a bowl and mix well. Let stand for 5 minutes. Combine the tomato juice, chicken broth, lemon zest, onion and parsley in a saucepan and bring to a simmer. Remove from the heat. Stir in the softened gelatin. Cool to room temperature. Strain through a sieve into a bowl, discarding the solids. Add the sherry, lemon juice, salt and white pepper and mix well. Pour into a 1-quart mold or small individual molds. Chill until firm. Unmold onto a serving plate. Garnish with the sour cream and chives.

YIELD: 8 SERVINGS

Nancy Reagan's Baja California Chicken

8 boneless chicken breasts
Seasoned salt and pepper to taste
2 garlic cloves, crushed

1/4 cup olive oil
1/4 cup tarragon vinegar
2/3 cup dry sherry

Sprinkle the chicken with seasoned salt and pepper. Heat the garlic in the olive oil and vinegar in a skillet. Add the chicken. Sauté until golden brown. Arrange the chicken in a baking dish. Pour the sherry over the chicken. Bake at 350 degrees for 10 minutes or until the chicken is cooked through.

YIELD: 8 SERVINGS

The Hermitage's Turkey Hash

This recipe was served to President Franklin D. Roosevelt, and also to Mrs. Lyndon B. Johnson when they had breakfast at the Hermitage.

1 large turkey
Chopped celery
Chopped onion
Melted butter

Sifted flour
Worcestershire sauce to taste
Salt and white pepper to taste

Combine the turkey, celery and onion in a large stockpot. Add enough water to steam the turkey. Steam until the turkey is tender and registers 180 degrees on a meat thermometer. Remove the turkey to a large platter. Chop the turkey, discarding the skin and bones. Strain the liquid from the stockpot into a container, discarding the solids. Chill until the fat rises to the top. Discard the fat. Combine the liquid with enough butter and flour in a double boiler to make a stiff sauce. Cook until thickened, stirring constantly. Season with Worcestershire sauce, salt and white pepper. Serve over the chopped turkey.

YIELD: 15 TO 20 SERVINGS

Old Hickory's Christmas

One of the most heartwarming affairs President Jackson, or Old Hickory as he was called, gave during his term was a memorable Christmas party for about one hundred Washington children. Jackson and his family played games with the young guests in the East Room. Afterward, the children were ushered to the State Dining Room for a grand feast of frozen fruits, candies, cakes, and fresh pastries.

Mrs. Lyndon B. Johnson's Spoon Bread

1 cup (scant) cornmeal
3 cups milk
3 eggs, beaten

1 teaspoon salt
1 tablespoon baking powder
Butter the size of a walnut, melted

Combine the cornmeal and 2 cups of the milk in a saucepan. Bring to a boil and remove from the heat. Add the remaining 1 cup milk and eggs and mix well. Stir in the salt, baking powder and butter. Pour into a greased baking dish. Bake at 350 degrees for 30 minutes.

YIELD: 8 SERVINGS

Betty Ford's Blue Banana Bread

1 cup (2 sticks) butter, softened
2 cups sugar
4 eggs
2 teaspoons vanilla extract
4 cups sifted flour
1 tablespoon allspice

2 teaspoons baking soda
1 teaspoon baking powder
1/2 teaspoon salt
2 cups fresh or frozen blueberries
5 medium bananas, mashed

Cream the butter and sugar in a large mixing bowl until light and fluffy. Add the eggs and vanilla. Beat at medium speed for 2 minutes. Reserve 2 tablespoons of the sifted flour. Sift the remaining flour, allspice, baking soda, baking powder and salt together. Add to the creamed mixture. Beat at medium speed until well blended. Toss the blueberries in the reserved flour in a bowl to coat. Stir the blueberries and bananas into the batter. Pour into 2 greased and floured 5×9-inch loaf pans. Bake at 325 degrees for 50 minutes or until the loaves test done. Cool on a wire rack.

YIELD: 2 LOAVES

Mrs. Lincoln's White Cake

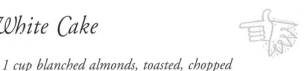

3 cups flour
1 tablespoon baking powder
1 cup (2 sticks) butter, softened
2 cups sugar
1 cup milk

1 cup blanched almonds, toasted, chopped
6 egg whites, stiffly beaten
1 teaspoon vanilla extract
1 teaspoon almond extract

Sift the flour and baking powder together. Cream the butter and sugar in a mixing bowl until light and fluffy. Add the flour mixture and milk alternately, beating well after each addition. Stir in the almonds. Fold in the stiffly beaten egg whites, vanilla and almond extract. Spoon into 2 greased 9-inch cake pans. Bake at 350 degrees for 25 minutes or until the layers test done. Cool on wire racks. Frost as desired.

YIELD: 12 SERVINGS

St. Michael's Church

In St. Michael's Church, Princetown, Devonshire, England, the NSUSD of 1812 installed a stained glass memorial window on June 4, 1910. It was dedicated to the 6,554 men who were imprisoned and to the more than 2,000 who died of their wounds or disease during the War of 1812.

Jacqueline Kennedy's Lace Cookies

1¹/2 cups quick-cooking oats
1¹/2 cups packed brown sugar
2 tablespoons flour
¹/2 teaspoon salt

¹/2 cup (1 stick) butter, melted
1 egg, lightly beaten
¹/2 teaspoon vanilla extract

Mix the oats, brown sugar, flour and salt in a bowl. Stir in the butter, egg and vanilla. Drop by teaspoonfuls 3 inches apart onto a foil-lined cookie sheet. Bake at 350 degrees for 8 to 10 minutes or until light brown. Cool slightly on the cookie sheet. Remove carefully with a spatula to a wire rack to cool completely.

YIELD: ABOUT 2 DOZEN

Note: These cookies have to be watched carefully. The cookies should be very crisp but if they are underdone or too hot when you try to remove them, they will be difficult to remove from the foil. If they are overdone or have gotten too cool, the cookies might crack. The cookies must be thin and come out almost transparent.

Cookbook Committee

Carolyn Drennen
Connie Grund

Martha Stanley
Carole Thomas

Contributors

Joanne Adams
Betty Aiken
Kitty Akins
Myra Avey
Virginia Bailey
Marjie Beatty
Kay Blankenship
Virginia Brown
Ann Carlton
Margaret (Peggy) Carr
Gwen Causey
Ann Hatchett Cheney
Jean Harmon Clark
Pauline Coppage
Lucy Hawthorne Currin
Coralie Davis
Stella Weaver Dillahunty
Allie Claire Dorough
Carolyn Drennen
Jean Edens
Mary Emma Fuller
Gethryn Giles
Connie Grund
Bettie Parker Gustafson
Evalyn Harris
Ellen G. Harwood
Peggy Holweck
Eula Jones Horsman
Norma Hulgan
Gloria F. Jones
Emma Jordan

Clarice Kennedy
Jessie P. Leonard
Marilyn Littlejohn
Lynda Logan
Rose Lotz
Janice L. McKay
Betty Fleming Marbert
Carolyn Martin
Betty Moon
Billie Ruth Moore
Mary Brabham Morgan
Dorothy C. Myers
Evelyn Morgan Nabors
Millie Patterson
Elner Pettiet
Barbara Pratt
Doris Richards
Aline Gray Roberts
Audrey Savage
Olyn Schnibben
Barbara Smith
Joyce Y. Smith
Karen Stanley
Martha Stanley
Margie Tucker Stewart
Carole Thomas
Margaret Thomas
Rena Underwood
Shelby Ward
Gretchen A. Warda
Leila Welch

Contributing 1812 Chapters and Societies

Alabama Charter Chapter

Colonel Thomas Hart Benton Chapter

Captain Johnston Blakeley Chapter

John Cavet Chapter

Cherokee Chapter

Brig. General John Coffee Chapter

General Clermont A. Evans Chapter

Captain James Gibson Chapter

Kaw Valley Chapter

Private Vincent Key Chapter

King's Highway Chapter

Colonel William Carroll Lee Chapter

General Alexander Macomb Chapter

Massachusetts State Society

General Patrick May Chapter

Nebraska State Society

Piomingo Chapter

Stephen Preston Chapter

Hampton Roads Chapter

Governor William Smallwood Chapter

Snap Dragon Chapter

South Carolina State Society

George Stake Chapter

Tippecanoe Chapter

Tulip Grove Chapter

West Virginia State Society

Wisconsin State Society

Index

Savor THE Spirit

3573 Rockhill Road
Birmingham, Alabama 35223
1-205-967-6954

YOUR ORDER	QUANTITY	TOTAL
Savor the Spirit at $22.95 per book		$
Alabama residents add 8% sales tax		$
Postage and handling at $4.00 per book		$
	TOTAL	$

Please make check payable to the Alabama Society 1812.

Name

Street Address

City   State   Zip

Telephone

Photocopies will be accepted.